WAYFARER MAGAZINE ISSUE 42.

FOUNDER AND EDITOR-IN-CHIEF

CONNOR WOLFE

SENIOR EDITORS

THEODORE RICHARDS

ISLA KIRKEY

HEIDI BARR

IRIS GRAVILLE

EDITORS-AT-LARGE

FRANK OWEN

THOMAS LLYOD QUALLS

KRISTEN WILLIAMS

ROBERT BRODER

WILL FALK

FRANCSCA G. VARELA

JOSE OSEGUERA

DAVID K. LEFF

contact us

WAYFARER MAGAZINE

PO BOX 1109, ABIQUIU, NEW MEXICO

WAYFARER@HOMEBOUNDPUBLICATIONS.COM

ORDERS@HOMEBOUNDPUBLICATIONS.COM

Since 2012, *Wayfarer Magazine* has been offering literature, interviews, and art with the intention to inspire our readers, enrich their lives, and highlight the power for agency and change-making that each individual holds. By our definition, a wayfarer is one whose inner-compass is ever-oriented to truth, wisdom, healing, and beauty in their own wandering. Our mission as a publication is to foster a community of contemplative voices and provide readers with resources and perspectives that support them in their own journey.

SUBSCRIBE AT SUBSTACK

We have some news to share! *Wayfarer Magazine* is expanding into a weekly digital publication. We've launched *Wayfarer Magazine* on Substack!

WWW.WAYFARERMAGAZINE.COM

FROM THE EDITOR

As a Queer/Trans-owned business, it is impossible for us to remain detached from the political climate. During these perilous times, I feel compelled to make our stance clear: Wayfarer Books and its imprints are firmly rooted in our vision of a compassionate, inclusive, and educated society, which we strive to promote through our publications. We are committed to progressive values, including support for LGBTQIA+ rights, trans rights, decolonization, women's rights, reproductive rights, non-violence, climate change science, freedom of speech, and the affirmation that Black Lives Matter.

At *Wayfarer Magazine*, we believe poetry is the language of the earth, a force that, like rivers through wild places, can change the shape of the world. We publish poets, writers, and renegades who stand outside of mainstream culture—voices fierce and unyielding, whose work might withstand the scrutiny of crows and coyotes, the crepuscular and the queer-at-heart.

Today, we face a world where fundamental rights and freedoms are under attack, and our mission has evolved to meet this urgent reality. With defiance and clarity, we stand against forces of oppression, using words as instruments of resistance. Through initiatives like *Voices of Defiance: A Series of Protest Poetry*, we seek to amplify voices that challenge bigotry, fascism, racism, and the suppression of marginalized communities.

Our books and publications are not just art, but acts of resilience and resistance—a map and compass for all who navigate wild terrain in the fight for justice. Wayfarer is more than a publisher; it is a community of storytellers, activists, and poets, united in the belief that words can illuminate darkness, provoke change, and demand accountability from systems of power.

We welcome all who are willing to speak out, to challenge, and to celebrate humanity in all its diversity. Together, through the power of poetry and prose, we create a resilient voice that refuses to be silenced.

With Deep Gratitude

—Connor Wolfe

(They/Them)
Founder and Editor-in-chief,
Wayfarer Magazine

At *Wayfarer Magazine*, "charting the way for change" has always been at the heart of what we do—an invitation to align with truth, wisdom, healing, and beauty as we navigate a world in flux. Yet, in the face of today's profound challenges—the erasure of marginalized voices, the ongoing climate crisis, and the alarming specter of violence and genocide—this phrase takes on new urgency. *To chart the way for change* now means more than introspection; it calls for boldness and collective action. It asks us to question the stories we've inherited, to amplify voices often silenced, and to seek paths that are not just compassionate but also transformative. As wayfarers, our journey is not one of passive observation, but one of deliberate, courageous steps toward a more just, sustainable, and inclusive world.

CONTENTS

FORKS IN THE CIRCULAR ROAD

BY STEPHEN DREW

I prefer the word *branch*. As in the branch of a tree. One tree, same wood, just a different shape from the trunk. Somehow, to fork, or split, or (God forbid) divaricate, implies the taking of a wholly different way. Experience has shown me there is only one path, a consistently circular one, though appearances might suggest otherwise.

> "Whether you turn to the right or to the left, your ears
> will hear a voice behind you, saying, 'This is the way; walk in it.'"

> — Isaiah, 30:21

It is May 2016, and I'm walking across the Spanish Meseta, a mostly flat, expansive high plain that occupies 225 kilometers of the Camino de Santiago in the midst of its 800-kilometer French Route. It is a heavenly place, with expanses of emerald-green grasses and new-growth wheat rippling in the springtime breeze, all under a fluid sky that's as big as the whole world. Across the emptiness to the north I see the Cantabrian Mountains, snowcapped and beckoning, though far too distant to approach. In the romance of the moment, I give them voice. They call me child and promise wonders beyond my wildest dreams. They seem wise and immortal and eternal, and so I believe them.

Not far beyond the city of Sahagun, I find myself at a place where the road branches. One path leans to the southwest, and one to the northwest, rejoining about 30 kilometers beyond. I'd known about this place before setting out today, yet the direction my feet would eventually find had eluded me. I walk northwest, the notion of choice noticeably absent, more an act of following.

As I walk the plain, I often gaze north toward the mountains with a deep curiosity about what it may be like to journey through them—an incipient longing, one could say. But for now, I walk the road before me, which, as it happens, is a Roman road. It was first laid during the time of Jesus, when it was used to transport gold from the mines of the Galician region across the Iberian peninsula. And so now there is the matter of time to be pondered as well. Also circular.

The surface of this road is actually but the substrate of the original, made of a mixture of coarse dirt and pebbles along with embedded stones that are a little smaller than a baseball. The events of time have removed the surface stones, leaving not a trace. Walking on it creates a full-bodied crunching sensation underfoot that travels through the soles of my shoes into my legs, finding its home in memory, still recalled with ease. That feeling, that sound, seared into my most essential place—forever things, and so now sealed away from the passage of time.

Near the end of the walking day, I arrive in what may be the loneliest place I've ever known: a village situated 8 kilometers from the last and 17 kilometers before the next, the distant mountains north, and nothing discernible to the south save for the horizon. It is siesta time, and I am alone here. I find my way to the southern edge of the village, remove my pack, and stare off into the void. Somewhere out there is the parallel branch I left behind, and a kind of sweet, benign grief wells up from all the possibilities there that would never come to be, much like during the joyful onset of new romance. I hear a faint train whistle carried on the wind from the high-speed railroad running between Palencia and Leon, too far away for me to see. My heart hurts with aloneness and the beauty of the great plain mottled by the shadows of fair-weather clouds. I'm left to wonder about who lives here behind the doors and shutters, and the love they must have for this place to transcend its isolation. I shoulder my pack and set off to find the accommodation my guidebook lists.

It is perched on the northernmost edge of the town, and my room offers an unobstructed view of the mountains. Perhaps my romantic sense is at work again, but there is an ineffable quality about this village and where it lies. I could envision living here, and even though I've journeyed a very long way along the Camino, I have not felt like this about anyplace else. As I sit at the window, I dream of a writing desk before me, words just rolling across the plains from the wise mountains directly onto my page. It has become a holy place.

The innkeepers are a married couple; the woman is softspoken and warm, her husband, gregarious and quite boisterous. I'm drawn more to the former, and during a quiet conversation later in the day, she confides a deep concern for the sustainability of their hotel on this northern spur of the Camino. For reasons she cannot understand, it seems most travelers are walking the other path, but as a couple, they remain committed.

"I feel we've been placed here," she tells me.

"I feel exactly the same way," I reply.

*

I had not written an artistically driven word in nearly thirty years. In my defense I can only say I'd become distracted with the noble effort of providing for a family, yet over time I wondered what happens to an ability left unused, an aspect of the soul unexpressed. Must such negligence be punished? Is there any hope for a return? My wondering had been a passive, idle thing until I came home from pilgrimage in late spring, from all the myriad branches that had been placed along its way.

Almost immediately, suggestions began to arrive in a rhythmic, repeated fashion through a series of seemingly chance encounters with several of those who'd known of my walk, suggestions that it was indeed time to place some words upon a page. A commotion ensued that compelled me into action. In what can only be framed as an act of faith, I returned,

or, more correctly, was returned. The first of those words began with a question, a wondering about the workings of time, about when anything really does begin. Time, as a theory, has a way of collapsing.

Four years later, from my imagined writing desk on the vast Spanish northern plain came my first published work, a tale of that very journey—time and distance and place left irrelevant. The words came steadily from the mountains, and at the end of each day's work, I'd review the words that had arrived with the sense of being the first person allowed to read them. The mountains are great. The writing voice through which the words appeared had been at rest for decades, but it woke as if no time at all had passed. The mountains are timeless.

*

Though I can't recall the source, I once read that the human experience in linear time unfolds as a series of roughly seven-year cycles. The idea seemed unremarkable, maybe even suspect, but for some reason it stayed with me....

It is the springtime of 2023, and I've been immersed in a period of reflection. A discreet-yet-persistent thought about one more ramble in Spain has risen. Another commotion is afoot. I envision two walking routes with two distinct intentions, two ways of rounding out this reflective chapter—one route through mountains, and one to the ocean. Perhaps in the interest of variety, I also see this as an autumn pilgrimage.

The ocean route immediately presents as a walk from Santiago de Compostela to the Atlantic at Finisterre, then up the coast to Muxia—a four-day, 120-kilometer trek with the intention of acknowledging grace. It feels settled, a perfect way to conclude the pilgrimage. But the other route is elusive. I contemplate walking the Camino Ingles from Ferol to Santiago but am feeling unenthused about it.

While messaging about this with a friend on Facebook, who, coincidentally, was introduced to me by a reader of my first book, he asks if I've ever considered walking the Camino San Salvador. It is a lesser-known route that tracks north from the city of Leon, traverses the Cantabrian Mountain Chain, and ends at the Cathedral of Oviedo, a distance of some 125 kilometers over five or six stages. He describes it as a stunningly beautiful route, but challenging as well, for crossing those mountains requires negotiating an elevation gain and loss of nearly 10,000 feet.

I feel as if I've been presented with another branch in the road, and I remember my old friend Isaiah. The voice behind me speaks, suggesting that walking here would perfectly fulfill my intention of penitence, and as if to offer a final punctuation, while viewing images of this lonely, often isolated route, I weep.

Flying into Spain from Ireland in early October, I arrive in the city of Bilbao. The following day, I board a high-speed train and cross the Meseta bound

for Leon. The sterile view from my seat brings a longing for the walk, for the thick crunching sound underfoot on the Roman roads, the windswept plains, the biggest sky I've ever seen, and for the distant mountain view. After departing the station at Polencia for the final leg of the trip, the train is cruising along as I hear the whistle sounding, and in that moment I'm returned to the loneliest place I've ever known, if only to hear its echo.

Dawn unfolds as I walk the two blocks from my hotel to Plaza San Marcos in the beautiful city of Leon. From here I am to begin the Camino San Salvador, starting at the feet of a statue on the plaza that depicts an exhausted medieval pilgrim at rest. I take a moment to consider what brought me to this place, at this time, this age, this condition of spirit, all of the various branches taken since those steps outside Sahagun seven years earlier, and all the branches that had led me to that one. This statue sits at the intersection of my first Camino and the one I'm beginning now. I've been here before; this medieval pilgrim is an old friend. Then, I'd headed west to Santiago. This morning, it's north to Oviedo.

On the first day, I move through foothills to the town of LaRobla and meet a walking companion along the way. Early next morning, we walk along the darkened streets and out into the countryside for a mostly level trek until reaching the village of Buiza. Under a clear autumn sky, the first of the mountain climbs begins, and soon we're transported to an otherworldly place of high meadows, craggy peaks, and mesmerizing views.

At the highest elevation of the day, we pause to rest. I take some steps away from my friend and turn to face toward the east and south. Before me is a vast, open valley, the mountain peaks continuing beyond. Past them lies the great Meseta, where I know pilgrims are walking their way, likely gazing north toward these mountains. Will some of them wonder as I once did?

Two days later finds me alone in the mountain village of Pajares, having bid a fond farewell to my companion, who needed to press on. The day before me begins with a steep valley descent, then a climb out. Seems simple enough, yet from the very first steps of the path down, a vague fear simmers.

There are many moments on pilgrimage when the road itself becomes personified. It insinuates itself in feeling, in thought, in word, and in action. I've even suspected this is likely a constant thing, that those moments are provided for the traveler to be aware of what always is. There is a crossroad ahead, and I intuit that the Camino may have a thing to say about this. A moment of reckoning is upon me.

I've allowed myself to run dangerously low on water and foodstuff, and still have 11 kilometers to go before reaching the day's destination, the town of Campomanes. After I leave the village of Llanos de Semeron and find no water there, the branch of the road presents. I knew of it even before I left home. At that time I'd decided to disregard the highly difficult mountain option and play it safe by staying on the road that courses mostly through the valley below. But now, I stand frozen here, staring at the single-lane path leading into the woods and up. I feel tears coming...the Camino's preferred language.

It is without mercy. Absent of words the voice speaks, conveying something like this:

Are you penitent, or are you not? Do you walk in faith, or do you not? Imagine for a moment, dear pilgrim, being home months from now after having walked the valley instead of the mountains. You looked toward the mountains long ago...did you not?

Sobbing now, movement returns and I take to the mountain route for the crucible that is to follow. In summer-like temperatures, I climb and sweat and thirst and hunger and bleed. I collapse and seriously wonder if I can go on. I come to realize I am becoming either a new man or a dead one. And with a little more than one kilometer remaining, I stagger into a hamlet—where I find a gush of cold running water. The Camino is as knowing as it is unmerciful. Alchemy delivered, the walk simply continues on to Campomanes and some blessed rest.

*

For the entirety of the Camino San Salvador in north-central Spain, I walked under perfect, clear skies and very warm temperatures, but because I know the various climates of the country, I'm aware that this is about to change. My walk to the ocean begins in Santiago de Compostela, capitol city of the region of Galicia. In mid-October, the weather here shifts into frequent, if not constant, rain, remaining that way for weeks. Still, the day of my arrival is sunny and warm, continuing through the rest day that follows.

On the day of my departure from Santiago, I awaken to the sound of wind-driven rain pelting the window of my room. I smile and say out loud, "Ah, Galicia. As it should be." Instead of dreading what lies ahead, I am delighted. It's good to begin a walking contemplation of grace by feeling this way. In fact, it is perfect.

Grace is sometimes hard to find. It has a way of concealing itself within this world of appearances. Sheets of driving rain could be seen as a distraction, but pilgrimage has taught me to notice more deeply. After a couple of kilometers, I clear Santiago's city limits. The storm has moderated somewhat from a torrential downpour. As I enter the forest, grace appears as the aroma of eucalyptus, now released by the Galician rain. Sweet and clean, it fills me to my depth. It will be with me for the remainder of the route, for eucalyptus trees are as ubiquitous here as the rains.

On the third day of this walk, (still) walking in a steady rain, I glimpse the Atlantic at last just before descending a hill into the fishing town of Cee. I'd been here on my first Camino, electing then to bus in from Santiago and walk the 13 kilometers from here to Finisterre. Passing the bus stop, I have the sense of completing a seven-year loop, a return, a continuance. After I stop for food and rest, the walk to Finisterre unfolds over familiar ground.

Cabo Finisterre reveals itself as it did before. From a point high above a long beach, I see the great finger of land pointing out to sea. Known as Fisterra in Gallego, the language of the region, it translates to end of the earth. After that first pilgrimage, I'd come here for nine days to walk and contemplate—to perhaps understand what had happened as I'd trekked across Spain from the Pyrenees Mountains of France. This time, though feeling nostalgic and planning to spend a day here, I'm mostly passing through. Another crucible awaits.

The notion of walking in a contemplation of grace along the Atlantic coast of Spain had an idyllic ring to it when it first presented as the focus of this walk. And by grace I mean everyday grace. Grace defined as the divine touch, the anointing of worldly life by its very own being, or source, or primal intention, its execution and timing nothing less than perfect; grace filtered out into the coarse, wild world from the unspeakably fine. Pure energy, sometimes as pleasant and gentle as an aroma, sometimes terrifying, always awe inspiring.

Windows rattle ominously in the hotel dining room, and the rainfall is a torrent. Before me I have a 31-kilometer walk up the Costa da Morte to the end of this pilgrimage at the village of Muxia. Grace it is, then.

Setting off with the heavy-duty poncho covering my 48-liter backpack, I look like a humpback hiker, lumbering along, ungainly. Adding to this is the effect of the wind gusts that stagger me as the pack acts like a sail.

My first stop, a detour, is on the moors of Castrominan, where I'd spent some days during my last time here. It is a pilgrimage within the pilgrimage. Then, these moors had been a refuge, a source of delight and inspiration, a mystical place that held revelation. But today that place is virtually uninhabitable in the storm. I return to the Camino route, an offshore tailwind pushing me away.

Later in the day, perhaps halfway to Muxia, the ongoing storm worsens. The wind is bending the treetops parallel to the ground and stripping bark; the rumbling howl of it is turbine-like and terrifying. Never before have I walked in the midst of something even remotely similar. In all of this there is a fear, not of death or injury, but of the message I know I'm being sent about my relationship with the very act of pilgrimage, a full-circle message in every sense.

Finally, I arrive in Muxia soaked and exhausted and a little angry, the day's walk and this October trek now finished, though pilgrimage is, of course, unending. Too tired even to eat, I get clean and dry, then fall into a defeated sleep.

Dawn's light bleeds through the windows, a brighter light than I've seen in days. The wind has laid down, now a mere breeze, and the rain has paused. The world has stopped yelling. I'm spending the day here before returning to Santiago by bus tomorrow for the first of two flights home.

After breakfast, I walk to the northern tip of the peninsula that is the town of Muxia. Reconciliation awaits.

I've settled into a nook among the boulders and ledges that make up the land here. The great Atlantic pounds ashore, the winds at the point noticeable but not overwhelming. I allow the sight and sound of it all to soak me through. The upheaval of yesterday's walk melts into peace and a clarity of thought reminiscent of the mountains' quieter moments. Through the choir of salt air, the eternal sea, its thundering waves, and the echo of every wayfarer who ever ended their pilgrimage in this place, I hear but one word spoken: goodbye.

There is a sculpture here commemorating an epic environmental disaster that occurred in 2002, an oil leak that wreaked devastation upon virtually the entire Atlantic coast of Spain. Named The Wound, it is composed of two large stone monoliths placed close together, the space between them seen as a jagged crack, open at the top. Certainly, it is the crack to which the attention is drawn, but for me there is something else.

I see two paths rising from the ground, a branching, and, for now at least, a departure. The alchemy of penitence has delivered a grace-filled goodbye to the idea of repeating the Camino, a dissolving of the external journey. In the end, it was always but a reflection—miraculous and luminous, but, still, a reflection.

Moving now into my final chapters, I'm ready to close out seven decades of living. Possessed of good health, optimism, and a rich, vibrant interior life, there is great promise ahead. Alchemy rendered, I am new. Grace delivered, I am returned.

I rise from my nook in the rocks and make the turn for home as any pilgrim should.

7

Stephen Drew (he/him) lives in a bucolic lakeside community in northwestern Connecticut. In addition to Around the Forever Bend, he also authored the memoir *Into the Thin, A Pilgrimage Walk Across Northern Spain* which was his first published work. Stephen practices a minimalist lifestyle which includes daily walking, mostly on the roads and paths near his home. Hiking there and elsewhere serves as a centerpiece of contemplative living and an ongoing awareness of Being. Visit him at: authorstephendrew.com

SHADES OF BEING

an essay by Shari Landeg

The doctors and Tibetan monk gather at the end of my bed, their urgent words, whispered, not to worry. Above them, a cloud-like substance floats just below the ceiling like a dark, depressive halo, edges lower and lower. I study it, wonder what it is and the answer comes immediately. Grief. It is their grief. And it hangs unhappily over their heads, waits to descend. I know now. I know that I am dying.

The monk comes to take my hand, his smooth palms puffed like new baby softness. Maroon robes waft spiced spiritual scents, smells that hold me, keep me present. He fumbles in his shirt front, offers me a handkerchief. I shake my head no, as I should have done three days ago.

We were part of a group retracing Siddhartha Gotama's footsteps to Bodhgaya in Bihar. One of the poorest states in India, one of the most sacred, the Prince spent seven weeks seated beneath a Bodhi tree absorbed in contemplative meditation, rising from his reverie a fully enlightened Buddha.

We traveled choked in dust, bandannas wrapped around our mouths and noses, our coach caught in a convoy of trucks that broke down, one after the other, after the other, traffic trailing a in long patient line behind us. Exhausted, we stopped for food.

The monk offered his plate of raw white radish, fresh cut tomato. Religious etiquette has taught me to accept what is offered by ordained Sangha. Unthinking him and me in that instant, when the uncooked fruit burst through my mouth, bittersweet.

Later, when I looked over the balcony to where kitchen boys worked the restaurants roadside trade, I acknowledged our thoughtlessness. A teenage boy squatted barefoot beside a bucket of black water. Clothes sizes too big hung from his slight frame. He saturated a filthy rag, stood, and wiped over a counter where food was being prepared.

I kept knowledge of our error, the boy's dirty act, quiet not to burden, a silence that festered known and unknown, deep in my gut.

In Bodhgaya that evening, nothing but the present mattered. Sunset descended in tones. A huge hand emptied a paint palette across the horizon, played about. Pastel finger streaks of mauve-pink and violet-blue, splayed across the sky. A tranquil calm draped over the village in heaven-time folds, peace palpable as the earth exhaled.

We spent time in the shadows of Mahabodhi Temple, seated as the Buddha had, the green sheltered grounds awash in maroon and yellow, as Tibetan monks and lay practitioners, prostrated in their hundreds. Under the Bodhi tree,

dappled in scented shadow, air flowed thick and heavy. Prayers and chants and muted laughter mingled to the soft, repetitive click of stone beads, floral and fruit and herbal scents, pungent and warm sweet.

I was the only Buddhist in our group, apart from the monk. There was a moment in the Temple interior, crowded with sweat and reverence, when our eyes met, the extent of our spiritual privilege, mirrored in the other.

Now, in this humble hospital cell, I grieve silently for what the monk may eventually realize—the deadliness of his gentle offering, extended with such quiet and generous humility. For the burden of a truth that will bow him low before his masters, those that teach the transitory nature of existence, impermanent, ever-changing. Truths that hover, present and real, unspoken in this room.

Life ebbs in subtle seconds. I can no longer feel my arms, the needles sharp metal tip repeating at my veins. A doctor bends close, blinks. The tips of her

lashes brush her eyebrows. A long plait falls over her shoulder, lies curled along the white sheet like a shiny black snake. Tension pulls at her face, casts deep dark shadows beneath her beautiful eyes.

Someone's breath soft and warm in my ear, "Do you want us to call your family?" Speech remains as thought only, unformed in my mouth as my consciousness, permeable, fluid, readies itself for flight. I turn away—there's no point worrying them yet, there's nothing they can do. To know would only cause them undue suffering.

I see them now—my husband and children, know the difficulty they will have accepting my death. The raw shock of it, their devastation. The pain and grief they will go through, not being here with me at this most crucial of moments.

But I know also that once their grief is unfettered from the emotion, and clarity has instilled itself in their minds once more, they will realize as I realize, that I could not have died in a more significant, more spiritually appropriate

place. I am in sacred Sarnath, just along the road from the Deer Park where the Buddha first turned the wheel of the Dharma. For a Buddhist, there is no better place to die. This realization, the knowledge that comes with it, brings a great, comforting, inner peace.

I visualize Green Tara, mentally construct the deities form, breathe her protective mantra deep into my lungs, hold on to the sacred syllables for a long, slow while, expel them gently through my nose.

Our teachers continually remind us that the enlightened qualities these beings possess are not removed from us. They are inherent within. Visualizing Buddha's such as Tara allows us to stimulate and activate specific qualities attributed to them, tap into this inner source when the need arises. Now, the potency of doing so is immediately apparent. I feel the deity's presence start to fill me with a strength I thought long past.

I close my eyes, sink into her mantra and when I open them sometime later, the monk is the only one left in the room. He sits on a warped wooden chair in deep meditation, face free of all concern. Behind his head, tired paint peels in thin grey shards. Still he sits beatified.

He senses I'm awake, opens his eyes, moves quickly from his chair, concern etched hard on his face now, "No need for worry, everything is being done to help you, everything possible, so don't worry."

I need to ease his fear, but it's still so hard to talk. I breathe deep and air comes, clean and temple tinged, flows and fills my lungs, forms and floats my words, "I'm fine, believe me. I'm at peace. This place...I am blessed to be here. You know this. You understand."

He nods his head slightly. But he still looks worried and confused now, lost to me somehow. Caught by the magnitude of the moment. And it fixes me. It fixes me more firmly to my physical self.

Energy comes now from somewhere beyond, rushes back into my body, a sparking pulsing charge so that I grab his arm, pull him close, breathe in his ear. "Should I not survive this, please do phowa."

Phowa practices are conducted by Tibetan Buddhist teachers who have been specifically trained to help people at the time of death. Different rituals, ceremonies and prayers are conducted over a 49 day period. Prior to, during and after death the consciousness is continually informed, advised and guided. Everything that can be done, will be done to make this transition as smooth, peaceful as possible.

For Buddhists, every moment is an opportunity for practice. Death is no exception, is seen as yet another opportunity for deepening ones spiritual practice and growth, is treated and treasured as such.

One's mental state at this time, is paramount, for it is only the physical body that dies, the consciousness continues on, journeying through various stages or bardos until its next incarnation. If the mind is unsettled or agitated, grasping to life, clinging to memories, transition can be fraught with difficulty. But if the mind is calm and at peace, able on passing to recognize its luminous clear light nature when that crucial moment becomes evident, then even at death there is opportunity for enlightenment, for great spiritual advancement.

Should I not survive this, it is important to me that phowa practice is done. Knowing there will be a teacher close to assist my consciousness as it begins the next stage of its evolution, is a great comfort.

I know the monk will honor my request. But I don't cling or grasp at that want now. If my karma is favorable, my request will be fulfilled. If not, then it is out of my hands.

I am happy and blessed to die in the shadow of Sarnath stupa, where the Buddha taught all those centuries ago. Ancient wisdoms which have informed, shaped my life. Now my death. The merit I have already incurred, that has led me to this sacred place, what will incur from this point on, is more than enough.

My request for the phowa ushers forth the monks understanding again. I see it in his eyes. A subtle shift, a remembering—our spiritual place, his and mine, here and now and other. He nods, smiles, his voice calm, "Of course, of course ...but please, have no concern. Just rest. Rest."

I look into him, know his goodness, and it fills me with a surging strength of love I cant define—not of this world almost. A powerful surging joy infuses my being. An elation that springs, fills me with a feeling of boundless energy, ripens over my face.

I tell him then, tell him why I'm not concerned—not at all. I tell him I have no fear. That this is what I have worked towards, what our teachings prepare us for. If I cannot put my practice into action now, then what has it all been for? What good fortune I have, to be here in this holy place, at this most tenuous, most sacred of times.

That I am blessed too, by his presence, here with me now.

Sharon Landeg (SHE/HER) received a B.A in English Literature and a B.A. Hons in Asian Studies from the University of Tasmania in Australia. She lives in Queensland, is currently enrolled as a corresponding student with The New Seminary in NYC and will be ordained in Interfaith ministry in 2014. Sharon has had poetry published in Australia in the Famous Reporter Literary Journal. This is the first time her prose has been published.

IMPERMANENCE, UNCERTAINTY, POWERLESSNESS

by Theodore Richards

In the year 1006, a star exploded. Visible for three years, it was observed worldwide, from China to the Americas, and is widely regarded as the brightest supernova in human history.

But there is something odd in the record of this event. It was far less noted in Europe than elsewhere, especially in the East. For it wasn't merely an explosion. It marked the first time in memory that the nighttime sky—the firmament—changed. And so, in spite of the fact that this was, in many senses, an event that was unifying—we all, after all, live under the same stars—it was perceived differently. This perception was colored by the worldview of the observer—that is, the extent to which a culture embraced change or permanence, certainty or the unknown.

The resistance to change is not surprising. Our world is filled with uncertainty. And this can be terrifying. For our earliest ancestors, the chaos beyond community, culture, and kinship could mean death. So they created not merely a space for physical safety, but also a culture that proffered the emotional security that comes from creating symbols and stories—a cosmology, which means both "beauty" and "order"—that give us a sense of place in the world, that give our lives meaning.

This is humanity's socio-cultural expression of what biologists call *umwelt,* what each species can perceive based on its sensory bubble. Every species is limited by its senses–humans, for instance, cannot see certain colors that birds can—but the umwelt is always experienced as all-encompassing. So too is this true of human culture, the symbolic and mythic worlds we construct. The world that most human cultures constructed was a dance between cosmos and chaos, certainty

IMPERMANENCE

Among the foundational philosophical debates of the Hellenistic world had to do with this question of whether to embrace change or permanence. The Greeks were consumed by the question of what is ultimately real. For Heraclitus (c. 535-475 BCE), the real was change. Nature, for example, is in a constant state of flux, creation and re-creation. His counterpart, Parmenides (born c. 515 BCE), however, insisted that the only thing that was real is that which is permanent. Everything else is an illusion.

In short, Parmenides, largely through the work of Plato and his successors, won. This notion of reality being changeless came to dominate the Western philosophical and theological tradition for centuries. They developed a theological worldview that emphasized the permanence of the spiritual realm, the divine and the soul. Their image of the cosmos emphasized the permanence of the stars. The quotidian world, the world of nature, was mere illusion. As a consequence, as time went on a civilization developed in Europe that was hyper-focused on control and predictability. It sought to engineer a better world than what nature had given us.

But there were other traditions that didn't follow this path. For Buddhists, permanence is an illusion. Indeed, the attachment to the changeless self—what Western theologians would call the soul, from the Greek "psyche"—is the ultimate delusion. It is not that we do not exist; it is that we exist only in relationship and flux, ever changing. Our attachment to this self is what leads to suffering.

UNCERTAINTY

One thousand years later another supernova occurred: The global COVID-19 pandemic. In addition to the obvious public health crisis, there was a corresponding mental health crisis. In part, this was in response to the deepening uncertainty in which we'd found ourselves. Of course, the pandemic didn't create uncertainty—it simply exposed it.

Our desire to impose greater control on an uncertain world was at least partly the cause of the rise of diseases like COVID-19, diseases that come from human encroachment on wild spaces. Indeed, our fear has led us to attempt to impose on the world a sense of order and control that has led us to devalue wild spaces altogether. We've not only damned rivers and sterilized soils, we have also attempted to sterilize and make-predictable human interactions and culture. We are at once consumed and consumer, algorithms rather than messy human beings. The dance between the chaos and cosmos has been replaced by a paved-over and sterile world.

The wisdom of this approach to life has now been called into question. While the pandemic has made us feel more acutely the lack of predictability and certainty in our world, the truth is that we never really were in control.

In my own life, I'd asserted control in ways of which I was largely unaware. I had lived my life "intentionally"—at least that's what I called it. I envisioned a particular kind of family, work, home, and career. But life tends to insinuate itself. Our children don't cooperate—whatever plans we'd had of them, they are autonomous beings who make their own choices. Careers ebb and flow in ways we cannot possibly predict. We are entangled in webs of choices we've made and cannot take back and forces beyond our control.

Throughout my twenties, I mentored young people. Recently, I've been replaying in my head a series of conversations I had with one young man, around the age of fourteen, who had a particularly hard life: foster care, abuse, poverty. He was a sensitive and gentle kid, but so angry. We used to talk about his life, about how hard it was, about the impossibility of changing certain things: it was the life he'd been given.

I've been thinking back to those conversations because I've been contemplating my own life. I'd been good at seeing the immutability of fate in the lives of others, but not for myself. The truth is that I believed that I could, to some extent, control my own fate.

I was good at talking others through this, but somehow missed it in myself.

POWERLESSNESS

Living through a global pandemic was fertile ground for all kinds of addictions. It was said that drug and alcohol use increased, for example. And it is here that we collectively might turn to the Twelve Steps. I'd never particularly given the Twelve Steps much attention. For me, they came across as a bit too theistic, gave a bit too much power to alcohol. And powerlessness? Are we really so powerless?

I can recall being sick overseas—malaria, altitude sickness, some stomach bug—in remote areas, without any possibility of finding a doctor. There, I did what people do, have always done, in such situations: I prayed. People don't, for the most part, pray because they necessarily believe in God; they pray because they recognize that they cannot control it, fix it. As they say in the Twelve Steps, "Give it to God." In other words, prayer is less about projecting power onto any idol—God included—than it is about humbling oneself in the face of an uncertain world.

The Twelve Steps can be implemented superficially, of course. One can exchange one addiction for another. Religion and God can be no less addicting than alcohol, albeit an arguably less harmful one. But at its core, the belief that we are in charge, that we can fix it with drugs or willpower or achievement, is the ultimate addiction.

The Buddhists would recognize this as a symptom of our belief in the immutability of the self. The Twelve Steps aren't really talking about alcohol as the ultimate problem. The ultimate thing we cannot control is, well, life. The ultimate addiction is to our own capacity to control.

*

These three things—uncertainty, impermanence, and powerlessness—lie at the heart of this collective, global teachable moment. We cannot know (uncertainty) or control (powerlessness) our world, because it is inherently relational and in flux (impermanence). Each moment is pregnant with possibility and potential, fraught with danger and mystery. Paradoxically, it is when we can be at ease with uncertainty, when we can accept our own powerlessness, we become free.

THEODORE RICHARDS (HE/HIM) is a writer, philosopher, and educator. He is the founder of The Chicago Wisdom Project and ReImagine Consulting & Coaching. The author of eight books, he has received numerous literary awards, including three Independent Publisher Awards and two Nautilus Book Awards. He lives on the south side of Chicago with his wife and three daughters. You can find out more about him and his work at www.theodorerichards.com.

FIELDWORK

by Stephen Trimble

A Selection from the anthology **Stories from the Trail:** *Field Notes on Moving through the Wild*

Walk out the door for... a walk or a hike? Or something else entirely? Hikes tend to be longer than walks, with elevation gain that requires effort. But if you aren't trying to clock miles, maybe the shorter hikes are really rambles.

For me, moving through space in my home territory at any speed always involves locating myself on an imaginary shaded relief map. I want to know where I am. There's no need to

watch that pulsing blue dot crawl across the Google maps screen. My screen is interior.

In this way, driving is just a higher-speed version of hiking—keeping track of biogeographic boundaries, looking for landmark features rising on the rim of the earth.

Here in Utah, it's the Henrys—last mountain range in the lower forty-eight to be named. Notch Peak, a nick in the horizon out west in

the Great Basin. Three scalloped cirques on Mount Nebo visible for more than 100 miles. Crossing the Colorado River at Hite, stopping on the bridge in the dark, listening to the steel beams humming, looking down and imagining the whole river basin stretching upstream to the Colorado Rockies and downstream through the Grand Canyon and on to the desert. Two hundred feet below the bridge, the river roils and purls and glides.

CAPITOL REEF NATIONAL PARK, UTAH | BY YUSIF

Naming these places, imagining their relationships, keeping track of my pinned spot on the continent gives me pleasure, grounds me. I'm moving across the earth, hiking on a grand scale.

Now zoom in with a whoosh to a single point, a single trail, still fully aware of where we are in space, in context. This version of hiking is more familiar.

My wife and I have a little house perched on a mesa in southern Utah. We've lived here for twenty years. From the kitchen window, red cliffs flare at sunrise and sunset, the ramparts of the Waterpocket Fold that provide Capitol Reef National Park its drama.

Midafternoon, we often say, "How about Chimney Rock?" What a gift to have this trail in our neighboring national park ten minutes from our home.

The scale retracts. Instead of that vast map of the whole West, this hike takes us across a single mesa on a looping 3½-mile walk. We know every turn.

First steps lead from the parking area through the Moenkopi Sandstone flats. Joanne says, "Don't run." We search for rhythm, then huff up the steep switchbacks into the easy headwaters bowl of Chimney Rock Canyon. The first trail sign—there are only two—directs us around the loop to the right. We prefer to go clockwise, contrary to the arrow's insistence. Down through what we call Cliffrose Wash, where the rangy shrubs blossom In early June, the high desert air spiked briefly with heady, honeyed perfume. Across the bare clay of Scalia Point, where Joanne once took a cell phone call from her sister with the news that Antonin Scalia had died.

Then a wide curving climb to the top of the mesa. Big views along the Fold. The ledge overlooking the landmark of Chimney Rock itself. A side hill where one crystalline winter afternoon we snagged first tracks in the snow, postholing all the way. Rimrock, ripple rock, slickrock. And down.

We stroll. We climb. We amble. We chat. We suddenly remember a dream from the night before or a new insight we've forgotten to share about a complicated family member. We watch the Wingate Sandstone change color with the light. Today the cliffs are burnt orange against flawless blue sky. Another day, the rock takes on the deep intensity of raw meat. Gray days mute the colors, tan to brown to violet.

We move deliberately where blocky sandstone requires caution. We speed up on smooth clay between gray and purple mounds of Chinle Shale. We swing into the downhill strides.

Every step is familiar. Every day is different. And the goal is to be there, to be outside, to use our muscles, to breathe, to return home exhilarated, for that beer I've been thinking about for the last third of the hike.

"That felt difficult today." "Today, it went super fast." "What fun to run into that wide-eyed young couple from Indiana." "How could that guy stay warm in that ridiculous outfit?"

That's a hike.

When I'm working on a book project, I call hiking "fieldwork."

I keep a tally of locations to photograph. I note places of ecologic or geologic interest. Special designations, special protection, "areas of critical environmental concern." These must be the spots worth visiting. I go to each one, solo, to write in my journal, to photograph, to experience, to add these places to the skein of descriptions, verbal and visual, that will bring the Desert West alive for readers.

When I go to Nevada, it's often for fieldwork. Just writing the word here makes me smile with anticipation. On this trip, my destination is The Table. First, I maneuver up a long rough dirt road to 10,000 feet, stopping at the weathered sign marking the boundary of the Mount Moriah Wilderness. Two miles of walking and a thousand feet up lies a tundra-like plateau, The Table, a sculpture garden for scattered Great Basin

bristlecone pines. All this, a thousand feet below the rubbly summit of Mount Moriah, Nevada's fifth-highest peak. There's no place quite like it.

This is my third time here, and I'm elated to return. Mount Moriah predictably yields useful material—the weathered trees for photographs, the mountain for context, the potential for bighorn sheep. And, for my journal, new language that may reveal the space, silence, and solitude of the Great Basin Desert. Fieldwork.

Especially when I'm working on a book, I remind myself: pay attention. I tick through my senses. I look for color and texture and light. I watch for stories, for telling details. When the light's too dull to photograph, I pull out my journal and look around, opening myself, doing my best to connect my brain to the place. Pen to paper.

*

Mid-afternoon I head up Big Canyon from camp, for I want to be on The Table at sunset, when the autumn supermoon rises. I'm not just hiking; I'm looking, intently. Closer and closer, smaller and smaller, the natural world transforms into an endless series of patterns. Aspen and fir on the facing hillside, a mosaic of textures. The path leading in suggestive curves between the white boles of the aspen. Leaves arranged in lovely compositions on the forest floor. A single crimson wild rose hip catching the sun. The contrasts of lichen on stone.

When I place the camera to my eye, it's both a window into the world and a barrier to full experience. I'm looking with more intention, but I'm circumscribing that vision. I've separated myself from unlimited connection, but I'm focusing with clarity and intensity on this one prospect seen through the viewfinder. Both ways of experiencing a place have value, both enrich me. But the difference is profound.

I shift each composition in my viewfinder, framing one graphic among a hundred that could be framed. The tenderness, the sensuality, the order of what I see when I simply deign to slow down and look thrills me.

I top out at The Table and turn off-trail to walk from tree to isolated tree. I can't help but move slowly, with respect, alone with the bristlecones. These are the earth's oldest living individual beings, living more than 5,000 years. They erode to sculpted twists of weathered wood, dense with resin, impervious to rot.

Like old people, they remain dignified—not lofty like sequoias but godlike nonetheless. Meditative rather than Olympian. Their best background music: occasional single piano notes.

The bristlecone's world is perfectly still, but my mind is racing. What's the best place to be when the moon comes up? Which snag will communicate the ancient spirit of the trees and pair gracefully with the moon?

I hear the air riffling the primary feathers of two circling ravens; the only sound. Last light turns my snag deep gold. The sky fades to pastels. "Sky-blue-pink," I say out loud, a perfect description I've borrowed from my mother-in-law. And, then, the moon. Huge, brilliant, rising right where I'd hoped.

I click my shutter, composing, recomposing, bracketing. I move forward, I move back, I crouch low in a dance that would surely look absurd to anyone watching. I crank up my tripod, I splay out its legs. I try to capture every photographic idea that occurs to me.

The golden glow on the bristlecone wanes. The sky is fading to black. I'm done. I put away my camera, turn, and head for my camp, leaving The Table in a hurry to beat the dark.

The downhill run is a hike, not fieldwork. I fantasize about dinner.

I leave behind two ravens, bristlecone pines, soft-edged evening stillness fast turning to night. And unseen, but satisfying, the possibility of bighorn sheep.

2
1

PETROGLYPH, CAPITOL REEF NATIONAL PARK, UTAH | BY RLW

HICKMAN NATURAL BRIDGE AT THE CAPITOL REEF NATIONAL PARK | BY CRAIG ZERBE

STEPHEN TRIMBLE (HE/HIM) grew up in the West with a geologist father who taught him that landscape has content. His 25 books are rooted in paying attention as he moves through his home territory, especially the deserts and canyons of the Southwest and Great Basin. He's won the Sierra Club's Ansel Adams Award for photography and conservation and The National Cowboy Museum's Western Heritage "Wrangler" Award. Trimble lives in Salt Lake City and Torrey, Utah.

LISTENING

TO OUR

LISTENING

by Gary Whited

Last summer I sat on top of Hurricane Point overlooking Silver Lake in central New Hampshire. Wind sounded through scant trees on the steep little hill mingled with the hum of a distant motorboat, then two of them. Their wake slapped against the shore at the foot of the hill. I heard its splash again and again until it went silent. Someplace deep in memory I heard the sound of wind on the prairie, how different it was from the wind here among trees and over water.

For every one of us there is a story to our listening. It started in some particular place, then traveled and evolved from that place and time to now. If we listen for it, we can hear the story of our own listening, and each of our stories differs from all others. Consider right now as you read this where your story began.

A storm seemed to be gathering over Silver Lake. I noticed the darkening air and the smell of rain. For a while the wind stopped, no boats passed by, yet my ears and my entire body kept listening. I thought to myself, does it ever stop? I've heard that hearing is the last sense to go when someone is dying. Maybe our listening keeps on going as near to the end as it can get, right out to the edge of breath. Maybe it dares to approach anything, any edge, any precipice. When places inside me get frightened, or happy, or sad at what I hear, listening goes on through it all, a vehicle for travel all around me and inside me.

As I look back over my life, all the way to its beginning, I recognize that my listening was taking its earliest shape by what surrounded me in that place of prairie, its many voices of wind from quiet breeze to fierce gust, the voices of all the creatures that lived there and became my first guides. As a boy walking the pastures this is what I heard:

NIGHT HAWK'S PATH

It happened the first time on the dirt cow path when I walked

behind the milk cow, evening chore-time light gliding across Shadwell creek

now shadowed for the night. When I stood still, that hum

no one ever talked about, coming from the earth, moved up my legs

into my hips, turning this body into sound. Light flared yellow,

gathered around haystacks, fenceposts, the cow and me.

Writing that poem opened my listening to the prairie again. Remembering earth's hum coming into my body as these lines came to me became its own kind of listening, bringing this hum back to me a second time as a gift.

The particular place on this planet that, for each of us, first shaped our listening stands amidst this larger place we inhabit together called cosmos by the ancients. Not only our planet earth, but all the rest of the solar system, our galaxy, and everything beyond, whatever that is, both what we know and what we don't know of it surrounds us, touches us on every side, shapes us and our listening in uncountable ways. Everything out there is coming at us, and everything out there offers its signal whether or not we have a name for it. I am compelled to imagine that a larger "hum" than even that of planet earth alone comes toward us always and in each moment.

Reflecting on my experiences on the prairie, where things and people came to me in tactile and visceral ways, I like to think that listening is close to touch in its essential nature. It invites into us whatever presses itself toward us on whatever organ of reception we offer. It can be our ears we offer to the words someone speaks, so we hear their story. It can be the heart we offer to the outpouring of another's grief as we hear of their loss. It can be the hand we offer to someone's reach for help, our mind that receives the imprint of another's idea, or the entire body that receives the invitation of a lover.

Though we think of listening most often as the experience of sound landing in our auditory capacity to hear, at its essence listening is receptivity, and we receive in many ways. That the hearing-impaired find other vehicles for listening than the auditory system testifies to this.

*

Listening happens in the call and response between those who participate in it and co-create it. A third "something" emerges when listening blossoms, and it carries the one calling and the one responding along a path they travel, trading call and response back and forth. When it ignites and is most alive, it is a kind of fire, its flames reaching for anything that offers something to be heard, and everything offers something.

There is nothing to do. Listening is the most natural response we offer to whatever being or creature in the cosmos calls to us in its way. The rattlesnake calls with its rattles ripping through the silence around its long body coiled in the bush when we walk past. We respond with our startle, our fear, our moving out of harm's way. The river calls to us with its murmur. We respond with our ears taking it in, and with our being moved by its gentle yet fervent whisper along its banks. Another person calls to us with her request for the salt shaker, for a helping hand, for an ear to hear her story. We respond with our ears, our hands, bellies and hearts, our touch and our willingness to be touched.

*

When our listening truly opens, it will almost surely carry us to something we don't yet know. Believing we know what's coming, we are less open. If we embrace not knowing, we might become aware of a silence inside, an absence of preconceptions. Not "listening for" what we already think we know, we might come into a stillness where we experience what Heraclitus, the ancient Greek philosopher, urges us toward when he says, "If you don't expect the unexpected, you won't find it."

But what about the times when our listening fails? When we fail to hear another, or we turn away from what the other is saying, what is happening then? What is missing? And what about all this time when we hear the news of our planet being destroyed by our consuming habits? How can we truly be listening yet still cascading toward environmental devastation? If it is so natural and easily opened to what is around us, how come it seems to close or be distorted at times?

I venture this. Our listening gets shaped in ways that constrain it, that warp it around a particular belief, an expectation, an agenda, or an old wounded place inside. When this happens listening becomes protective. It closes at the places where some part of us is trying to steer away from an unwanted feeling or thought. This happens both on an individual and a collective level. Our culture, our patriotism, our religious or scientific orientation, political persuasion, personal agendas, historical traumas, all of these shape and constrain our listening. We see this in the strife of the world today, in the war torn Middle East or Ukraine, in the fight for environmental sanity, anyplace where intense and polarized activity erupts in the absence of open and responsive listening.

*

It can be more subtle than these examples. Even our agenda to help someone can constrain our listening, turn it into an instrument we are trying to wield rather than an open vessel ready to receive another's call. I practice psychotherapy and at times my desire to help my clients does affect how I listen. When I take myself to be an instrument of healing, I'm less a healer. I've learned that if there is anything to do to enhance my listening, it is to listen with compassion and curiosity to those very places where I am vulnerable and protective and where some door might be ready to open.

IN THIS BODY

There are rooms that close their doors. Years pass
and a breeze moves through.
Maybe it was the look of that man with red hair and heavy hands,
or the woman crossing the street with the soft fingers and far away stare.
A door blows open slightly, the hinges barely agree. Behind that door
there's a small child who wants you to call him by name.

In my work as a psychotherapist my first task as I enter into relationships with clients is to listen ongoingly to my own listening. My next task is to guide clients toward listening to theirs, to help them discover where it might be blocked yet ready to open, ready to receive the call from a scared or lonely part of them who wants to know that someone is there, finally, and listening.

I try to remember as I sit down to each session that I could approach it as I would a poem I've not heard before, and that I want to hear the poem in its own terms, to be open to its voice and what it might reveal to me. When my listening as therapist opens in this way, I feel myself leaning in more, noticing subtle changes in the tone, the gaze, the posture; tracking this person's story as it unfolds through voice and body. A deepening curiosity guides me toward what is ready to show itself

When a client responds to the invitation, there is and there is not a therapist and a client. While I might be the guide at times, what really happens is two people listen to each other, bear witness each to the other. It is a profound event when it happens, and the two of us do not leave the same as we entered. Something has called us toward that boundary where our knowing borders our not knowing, opens us to the unexpected in the face of which we are likely to feel vulnerable, excited or both. If we keep listening there, places in us begin to appear that haven't been heard maybe ever, and what they reveal guides us further along the way. This is also where, if ever we do, we're likely to receive some kind of guidance from sources for which we don't have names, at least not yet.

This applies beyond the psychotherapy dialogue, to countries at peace or at war, to parents and children, to relationships of all kinds, and to all of us together in our struggle to save our natural environment. Let us listen to each other as well as to what the river says, what the tree says, the sky and the field, all of it.

In any dialogue witnessing grows out of this listening to our listening. This might be the most profound agent of change we have as humans who speak, who grieve, who weep and laugh, who offer to travel with another to yet unknown places. A few lines of a poem from Rumi speak to this:

"Talking can be sweet. A field can bloom in your Eyes when sharing words with the right person. ...

Find some ears that love the touch of your Sounds, and you theirs."

This is what we have to offer one another, nothing more and nothing less. Our authentic and open listening reveals more of who we essentially are, each of us to ourselves and to one another. It is a profound offering, it is fierce and it asks everything of us.

2
7

Gary Whited (he/him) is a poet, philosopher and psychotherapist. His first book titled, *Having Listened,* won the 2013 Homebound Poetry Prize. In 2014 it received a Benjamin Franklin Silver Book Award. His poems have appeared in journals, including *Salamander, Plainsongs, The Aurorean, Atlanta Review,* and *Comstock Review.* Gary lives in Boston, Massachusetts.

IN THE NARROWS:

LASCAUX II AND THE GEOGRAPHY OF HOPE

ESSAY AND TEDX TALK BY LESLIE VAN GELDER

From the *Wayfarer* Archive, 2015

When the replica of Lascaux was built into a low hillside near the original cave in Montignac, France, a decision was made to reverse the 'sense of the visit', so that the visitor would arrive immediately into the grand Salon of Bulls and be brought almost instantly into the majesty of the art. While a small interpretive chamber precedes entrance into the cave and allows the guides a teaching space to dispel myths and create interest for those who have come simply because in both senses of the word, on a summer's day they have heard that the replica is "cool," the immediacy of arriving in the Salon often leaves people breathless from the shock of being in the presence of so much art and at such a grand scale. At the Sistine Chapel, to which it is often compared, one has already walked the whole length of the Vatican to get there. In Lascaux II it is immediate.

The chamber itself is large and oblong with the shape and feel of a Viking longhouse. Along the high walls run black shadow horses who meet a delicate tribe of deer, their antlers filigreed like tree branches held up on heads raised as if they are sniffing the wind across a snowy plain. Above them thunder spotted white bulls for which the hall is named. White bodies born of limestone brought from the walls by hands holding black manganese with such certainty that the bulls leap from the walls themselves, their legs suspended in flight. In the cacophony of images, some 130 in all, the overall sensation for me has always been an auditory one. Absent the true red bellied Chinese horses and the black shadow sprayed true auroch's bodies, I hear their hooves and feel their bodies as if I were in the midst again of the wildebeest migration in the Serengeti I once experienced as a fugue of hooves, horns, and dust, when I was a child.

The guides, conscious of time and the next tour which must begin promptly at *quatre heure* talk through the whole visit. They use their red laser pointers to show the ways in which the artists outlined the shapes of some of the larger animals before they sprayed ochre, probably ground up in their mouths and then either spat in a pattern like our modern day spray paint cans, or through a bone or reed straw for far more accuracy. The skill in the artistry alone is dazzling.

For those for whom this might be their only visit to a cave or a painted cave, the guide's curation of the exhibit, not unlike taking the tour at the Met, might feel just right. For me, though, after years of working in neighboring caves where we have the time to be able to move more slowly through and to take in not only the images, but the images set inside the soundlessness of the space itself, and to be able to feel the vibrations of our voices set off from the cave walls, it is a very different experience. At Lascaux II on a Sunday at the height of summer tourist season, I couldn't hope for such resonance.

And yet, we had been lucky. I had brought a group of friends who had been together at a conference in western France for a few days of seeing the caves in the Dordogne. We had arrived late and our tour was the last tour of the day. The group was small, and because our group included two interested adolescents whose response to the cave was so palpable, the guide took her time, letting us linger in the Salon before leading us down into the Axial gallery below.

On previous tours with larger groups of people, visiting the Axial gallery had been as pleasant as the London Underground during July rush hour. While the walls of the Salon of Bulls are wide and expansive, in the Axial gallery, the feeling of the narrow stream that would have carved the cave becomes apparent. High walls rise in tight and the floor slopes gradually downward towards the image of a falling horse. Above, the ceiling floats with the bodies of ochred aurochs, horses, including my favorite – a tiny blown black horse tucked innocently into the wall, like a toy left behind after a family who had lived there for 5 generations had sadly moved away. A deer with antlers that in life would have weighed hundreds of pounds graces the right side wall with its graceful head up, facing the wind. Its long back is a single uplifted calligraphic stroke.

Because the walls come in so close and at a height that gives the feeling of being corralled by palace guards, the only place to look is up. In that, the sense of the passage and the art flowing through it is as unmistakable as the feeling one has standing beneath the Milky Way as it curves westward across the night sky.

On this June trip, as the guide was in no rush, she let us stay in the Axial gallery in a spot I would call the Narrows for long enough for the group to grow quiet and simply feel the space. With the vibrations from our voices finally quieting, the closeness of the walls produced a feeling in my chest I knew from the past the feeling of grief. A sort of heartache that has in it both all of the sadness I feel tangled in the colors of joy.

"You feel it?" she said quietly to me in French.

I nodded. "What is it?"

"I do not know," she shrugged her shoulders in the way only French women can do to convey so much with the same simplicity with which a deer's whole body had been expressed by a cave artist in single line. "But, I do know this. Even here, in the replica, sometimes, if we stop here for a moment too long, someone in the group will begin to cry. I do not know why."

She paused for a moment and then began to speak again, more slowly and in English for the benefit of the others who were listening to us.

"The cave, as you know, was discovered in 1940 during the war. It was opened to the public officially in 1948, but in the years after the war many of the survivors of the camps were brought here by the government to see Lascaux. The sense of the visit was different then, so they came through this gallery first and then up into the Salon of Bulls.

The guides who took these groups told me that the experience of the visit with these people was always the same. They would come to this point, where you are standing now," she gestured to me," and they would look upwards to the animals on the ceiling of the Salon of Bulls and then from nowhere within them they would weep and weep as if they could not go on."

One of the men in our group asked her if she knew why this was, and she looked round at the closeness of the walls that could feel like the shoulders of prison guards, or perhaps in a group could evoke the tightness of a railway car going into the dark unknown, and yet when one looked up at a gift of art so clean, so absent of humanity except to have been made by human hands shining above like stars undamaged on a summer's night, she said, "It is something in the soul. I cannot say. I know only this, that even here, in a replica made only 30 years ago, there are people, like you, who feel what is here, and you, too, you weep."

"Come, we should move on."

She motioned to the head of the group to move out past the falling horse painted in an apse in the wall, its body curving downward round a corner of stone, disappearing into darkness.

I looked backwards to the now fading light of the chamber behind us and then followed the others through the absent river of stone, grief still pushing against my chest while above, a tiny black horse stayed behind, as it had for 17,000 years, waiting for the next returning pilgrim to notice its perfect muzzle set against the high stone walls.

Five years before that visit to Lascaux, I had been in the Narrows life had created without the benefit of limestone walls and underground rivers. Instead, the Narrows had been born of cells in my husband, Kevin's body. Cells that had chosen to become a variety of non-small cell lung cancer and, like the river, had carved out a tumor sized space in the left side of Kevin's brain. There, perhaps in their own way, they were creating chambers emptied of life that could one day be populated with ochred hands and fire bellied horses. For us, in the summer of 2007, our world narrowed down to the geography the cancer created in our lives. Our world travels became limited down to the daily bus trips to Oxford's Churchill hospital where, over a ten day span of daily radiation to his brain, we followed the bloom cycle of a pair of twinned lilac bushes, one white and the other deep plum, which we religiously stopped to sniff on our arrival and departure from the bus stop every day. A stalwart blackbird perched on a Norfolk pine in a neighbor's yard and Kevin never failed to greet the blackbird and ask it about its day. And then, each day, with a little less strength than on the previous, Kevin would hold my hand as we walked into the hospital where a grey plastic mask perfectly molded to his proportions like a death mask of yore, would be put over his face while he was attached to a table, utterly unable to move, but still able to breathe, while a high dose of radiation was delivered directly into his brain.

I was not allowed to accompany him into the radiation wing, so I sat with the same group of people, who, like the fellow travellers in the Canterbury Tales, were bound to each other, each carrying a story and each on an individual version of a strangely same pilgrimage to the land cancer had created. This being Oxfordshire, we examined each other's shoes surreptitiously to answer unspoken questions about class, as one couple wore beautiful bespoke leather shoes highly polished even while he became more ashen by the day, while two others, wore the sturdy industrial shoes given out at a pensioner's home. In the days ahead we enquired on the basics of life – had you had a good night (no one ever answered this one honestly, nor did I), the traffic on the A34 (always shocking and worthy of shaking one's head about), and the deep comfort found in a good cup of tea (which though never spoken but was always clearly thought that is should be able to cure everything in life that ails one, including cancer). If not, this radiation business, would be the next best thing, though there was really nothing like a good cuppa and a Belgian bun, now was there?

Kevin would emerge from the radiation wing holding onto his new walking stick, swaying a little, and ask if we could go find a cup of tea at the hospital canteen. I would bid farewell to our

fellow pilgrims til the next day and we would take the old metal lift up to the canteen where white haired women hefted pewter kettles (no doubt also leftovers from the war and still perfectly serviceable, thank you) filled with proper leaf tea. Kevin would drink his cup, then mine, then get another, and then we would begin the slow trip back home again, where on the bus or over the tea, or climbing back into bed at home, he would tell me of the purple colors he saw while the machine shot his brain full of light. After he was sure he could smell ozone in the air, the same smell he had told me he remembered from his childhood when the ocean waves beat against the stone walls of the New Plymouth jetty or the scent he remembered of the wild waterfalls of Iceland's Gulfloss.

Later in the month that followed the radiation, he slipped into cavernous spaces within his own mind where he was sure that we had a cat (we didn't), that the time we were living in was named Elizabeth, that 3:45 was yellow and 4:30 was pink, and that his toes should be hereafter referred to

as Number 3. He slept or dozed 23 hours a day and could barely eat when offered food. In the span of eight weeks he eroded from being a vibrant and brilliant man to one who told me that there were disc shapes and baguette shapes in his brain and that his job each day was to sort them into the right categories and make sure that he put them all away correctly. In his own way that summer he must have been re-cataloging his brain, and while some pieces disappeared, never to return again, much did return and by mid Autumn he could eat a little again and the synesthesia had faded along with the discs and baguettes. Instead he was writing archaeology articles, planning his next book, and learning how to walk unaided again.

As Kevin's world diminished that summer, and all possibility of having a life that had any form of predictability to it, I wrote to a friend trying to capture how I felt. The immobility of our life and Kevin's illness pressed in at me from one side saying that we could have no future plans and we had to inhabit a constant state of "now." The need to keep my job and maintain an

income for us pressed in from the other side. And my belief that I wasn't doing my 'real work' of being a writer, pushed in from a third side. From other directions I felt the weight of being soul caregiver and morale booster and felt little support in the way that I needed. I now believe that it truly does take a village to support a caregiver who is carrying not only the physical needs, but the emotional weight of sustaining a dying person's optimism. Optimism and hopefulness are beautiful things but they require far more energy to maintain in the face of despair than one would think.

Across from our bed was a bookshelf built into the wall that held some of my favorite books. I looked to these authors - Barry Lopez and Robert Penn Warren, Rainier Marie Rilke, and Mary Oliver—as if they were old friends and middle of the night companions. When my friend wrote to ask how I felt amidst all of the pressures that life had produced in such abundance in the same way the cancer had proliferated with abundance inside of Kevin, I told him that I felt like a slim volume of poetry on my bookshelf. Sparse, as good poetry always is—just the essentials and nothing more.

Later, in the days just before Kevin died, that same friend would tell me that I reminded him of beach glass—my edges made softer by the relentless battering of the waves—but that what was inside of me had become luminous, and through the softness of the glass I glowed.

That was still a year to come. For now, I was a thin volume of poetry. I was my faded green copy of T.S. Eliot's The Wasteland eking out an inch of space between the Snow Leopard and Crossing Open Ground. I had bought Eliot for a course in early modern Arts and Ideas during my first year at university. My mother died days after I purchased it and in the November darkness of my first foray into the landscape of grief, I had little to light the way, save for Eliot's poem which spoke to the cacophony of fragmentation I found inside myself that year.

I did not take the poetry from the shelf as the books around it were wedged in so tightly that to move one was to collapse them all and in some strange way I felt I would be letting down all of those stalwart writers if I were to move them from their companions. On sleepless nights I read J.K. Rowling's

Harry Potter books over and over simply because she had created a perfect world which resembled this one, but like the experience, I, too, was having, her world had far more to do with things like Honor, Love, Fidelity, Truth, and the wonders of Magic, than the world of pewter tea pots and machines that could turn a man's brain from something whole to a time period, we could only call, at his insistence, Elizabeth.

Words from Eliot's *Wasteland* were so familiar that I found them within me whether I meant to invoke them or not. His gift was the expression of the fractured nature of a landscape attempting to grieve itself. Like our April of the brain tumors that year, his April was the cruelest month "breeding lilacs out of the dead land, mixing memory and desire," while our hospital lilacs mixed with the purples of Kevin's radiated brain, and I was like Eliot

at Margate Sands holding on the feeling as it slipped through my fingers, "I can connect nothing with nothing —" and in the end felt like a heap of broken images kept together by the confining space of the pressures on all sides, which at the time, held me prisoner to a futureless immobility, but also were a great kindness, for once free of the pressures through Kevin's ultimate death in 2008 (Shantih, Shantih, Shantih, says Eliot) I did not feel myself to be the luminous sea glass my friend saw but knew myself to be the fallen scaps of self that now, absent of what bound them together in the collective support of Kevin, flew off like winter street corner leaves subject to every slight or gust of wind that blew my way.

In the Narrows in Lascaux, I wonder now, did the survivors weep because they felt safe being held by the closeness of the walls and their companions

and the familiarity of it all having been held together by the pressure of outside forces? Did they fear, just a little, just as I did, the dissolution that would come in the suddenness of open space?

Or did they simply weep because their experience of humanity had not allowed, for so long, the creation or belief in so much beauty?

Perhaps that alone is enough in this world to make one keep believing that there is something beyond the narrows, something that even in the darkness of a cave, opens up into the light.

Leslie Van Gelder (she/her) is an archaeologist, writer, and educator based in the Rees Valley of New Zealand. Author of Weaving a Way Home, she studies lines people drew with their hands on the walls of prehistoric caves in France, Spain, and Australia. Her work has been featured in *Irish Pages, Earthlines, Antiquity,* and the *Bellevue Literary Review* and a TEDx talk on the *Archaeology of Intimacy.* She is a member of the College of Education Ph.D. faculty of Walden University.

TERRANEXUS

CONNECTION AND MEANING IN ORDINARY PLACES

AN ESSAY BY DAVID K. LEFF

IT TAKES A MAN OF GENIUS TO TRAVEL
IN HIS OWN COUNTRY, IN HIS NATIVE
VILLAGE; TO MAKE ANY PROGRESS
BETWEEN HIS DOOR AND HIS GATE.

—HENRY DAVID THOREAU,
JOURNAL, AUGUST 6, 1851

I. SUDDEN ONSET TERRANEXUS

In the heart of New Hampshire's White Mountains, I took my first steps up the well-worn Crawford Path. It was the beginning a solo trip across the Presidential Range with stays at the legendary high huts of the Appalachian Mountain Club.

Intoxicated by spicy spruce air, eager for the steep climbs promised by the map's clustered contours, I passed a yellow Forest Service sign warning of bad weather, danger and even death above tree line. This only fueled my teenage rite-of-passage dreams, and the white Appalachian Trail blazes stirred an urge to walk from Georgia to Maine. Here on America's oldest recreational footpath, cut in 1819 by rugged hostler Abel Crawford, I felt my journey somehow connecting with generations past. It was my first adventure in the wild, and I was ready for a test of manhood. What I was not prepared for was to discover an entirely new way of experiencing landscapes.

Although the first day's hike to Mizpah Spring Hut was only two-and-half miles at a relatively easy grade, the 1,900-foot elevation gain exhausted me. I nevertheless became reenergized on reaching my destination in the windswept col between 4,000-footers Mts. Jackson and Pierce. Maybe it was the bracing alpine air, the anticipation of climbing to the bare rocky tops the next day, or just a novice's sense of accomplishment. I reveled in conversation with fellow hikers, swapping stories over the hut crew's homemade soup and fresh-baked bread, listening to old timers telling heroic and humorous tales. I also made a brief raid on the small library of well-thumbed books, soaking up history, geology, ecology and lore.

The next day offered stiff breezes and azure sky dotted with clouds. Along the ridge, astringent light revealed a roiling sea of green slopes punctuated with ashen ledges that seemed to break like ocean whitecaps. The trail moved through small trees, krummholz thickets, and lichen-crusted rocky plains where hardy mountain plants grew in tufts and low mats. I was gripped by the powerful natural grandeur, and the path marked by crude cairns and sometimes edged with stones seemed to possess the nobility and timeworn quality of a Roman road.

While my senses feasted on the on the stark and cragged terrain, my imagination wandered in time as well as space to Indian legends, grand hotels, logging railroads, wildfires, home-crushing landslides, rare flowers, and ancient continental crashes that formed the mountains. Not limited merely by what I saw at any given moment, I encountered

a richer, denser world. It was love at first sight. I felt a sudden, strong attachment, manifestation of a phenomenon I've since called "terranexus," profound connection to terrain or place.

I'd fallen in love with places before, just never so suddenly. It was usually, even at such a young age, by long association—the wooded lots I wandered in the suburbs at home and my great uncle's New Jersey chicken farm among others. But this time my infatuation was clear and precipitous.

We spend time in places like the White Mountains for recreation, physical challenge and to find respite from an ever accelerating frenetic life. This "land of many uses," as the U.S. Forest Service has called our national forests, has been set aside for scientific study, wildlife, timber harvests, hunting and fishing, clean water, and to protect geological marvels and historic sites. But while these practical reasons support conservation initiatives and appropriations, they tell a junior part of the story. After all, many other places boasting such values remain unprotected. Ultimately, the political, financial, and social will to create and maintain the White Mountain National Forest and areas like it results from deep affection by small cadres of activists and wide swaths of the public.

Federal legislation, layers of management plans, wilderness designations, and all the hard work that has gone into creation and maintenance of the forest are perhaps less the result of science, resource management needs, recreational desires, and tourist dollars than it is a matter of love, attachment of people to a place. And it's not just woodsy quiet or the austere beauty of summits that stirs such passion, but a history of human interaction from Native Americans to the pioneering Crawfords, from the cog railway to the hut system to the Mount Washington Observatory.

If we are to protect wild areas as disparate as Labrador and the Amazon from invasive species, encroaching development, climate change and other threats, it will take terranexus, a revival of connection and romance between people and places. And it will require not just a fondness and devotion to distant and wild locations, but to nearby and built environments where our attitudes toward land are formed. Only by appreciating, understanding, and improving the everyday landscapes in which we live and work will we be able to ensure the future of the White Mountains and other places where nature is dominant and human beings feel like visitors. The close-to-home areas where we first learn about the outdoors "are places of initiation," ecologist and author Robert Michael Pyle has written, "where the borders between ourselves and other creatures break down, where the earth gets under our nails and a sense of place gets under our skin. They are the secondhand lands, the hand-me-down habitats where you have to look hard to find something to love."

After that first White Mountain journey, I longed to recapture the happy endorphins of falling in love with a place, the adrenalin rush of sudden onset terranexus. But with life becoming busy as I progressed into my twenties, it was increasingly tough getting to remote, untrammeled destinations. So I began exploring close to home, finding near-at-hand places more alluring and intriguing than I had ever imagined.

Maybe it was my youthful delight in doing something contrary and unexpected, but I itched to canoe western Connecticut's once famously and hopelessly polluted Naugatuck River. Though it was nearby, it was a kind of terra incognita for paddlers. No one I questioned had attempted it. "Had hepatitis shots?" I was asked half jokingly by friends who knew the river's reputation. Then, sensing I was in earnest, they stared with a chilling mix of concern for my safety and wonder at my sanity. Naugatuck River water carried disease, I was warned, hid submerged metal objects that could slit the toughest canoe hull, and was laden with unmarked dams that remained invisible until too late. With a bit of trepidation, I pondered the warnings and the opportunity for years before finally dipping my paddle in the forbidden waters.

Until little more than a generation before my journey in the early 1990s, the Naugatuck had been the nation's center of brass manufacture for over a century. Along the river's banks, the metal was forged from copper and zinc and fabricated into clock parts, kettles, buttons, buckles, tubing, hinges, artillery shells, wire, gears and automobile parts. Over time, the swift waters became an open sewer for industrial acids, dyes, heavy metals and human waste. As early as 1899, a government report found that the river had reached the limits of permissible pollution. A 1966 survey found not a single fish alive in its 39-mile length.

Once actually on the water, I found a world of startling contrasts. The river flowing past wild-seeming banks lined with silver maple,

sycamore and cottonwood where black ducks, mallards, mergansers, and geese floated, also rushed through small, gritty cities with fortress-like factories sprouting stacks, vents, exhausts and intakes. At one point I passed a maze of pipes and tanks at a chemical plant and then suddenly found myself in a constricted valley of tumultuous rapids where ospreys and turkey vultures soared above steep forested ledges. Near where drowned shopping carts and piles of bald tires collected like suicides, I spied muskrats and freshly peeled beaver chewed sticks turning slowly in eddies. Sewage treatment, control of industrial discharges, and the closure antiquated factories were resulting in rebirth of a river once shunned and given up for dead. Water quality has gotten even better in the ensuing years. Over thirty species of fish are now at home in the Naugatuck.

Despite some trash along its banks, and passage through densely developed urban and suburban areas, I found the river beautiful, not only for where it went, but for where it had been and where it was going. A place that was once a joke had become a source of inspiration and fun eliciting joyful, not derisive laughter. I was struck by *terranexus* in this debased and degraded place, not just because of unexpected natural beauty, but because its long and tangled encounters with humanity added layers of intrigue.

My Naugatuck voyage spawned a new interest, affection almost, for the hard used places where civilization and nature are entangled. About a mile from home via a walk wholly on pavement, such a location became my "listening point," a place where I can be wholly within myself and both contemplate the grand mysteries of the universe and mundane conundrums of daily existence.

The term "listening point" was coined in the title of naturalist Sigurd Olson's 1958 book, a paean to his special place, a bare glaciated spit of rock at the water's edge in northern Minnesota. Each time he went there it "opened

great realms of thought and interest" where he saw "the immensity of space and glimpsed at times the grandeur of creation." He christened his spot "listening point" because "only when one comes to listen, only when one is aware and still, can things be seen and heard."

My listening point is neither remote nor secluded. It's a mere fifteen-minute walk from where I live, a place where sometimes hundreds of people pass daily on foot, bicycles or roller blades. But, I can be there easily, at the slightest whim whenever the day gets hectic or the spirit moves me. Until little more than half a century ago, most of my walk to this spot was a corridor for locomotives hauling freight. The site itself was a hydroelectric station. But as Olson observed, a listening point does not have to be "close to the wilderness, but some place of quiet where the universe can be contemplated with awe."

From this perch on the west bank of Connecticut's Farmington River at the lower Collinsville Dam, I often sit on one of the rusted I-beams embedded in the concrete abutment that once served as a gate structure to bypass water. It's surrounded by trees, offering a commanding view of riffles downstream and the dark, glossy impoundment above. Across the water are a moldering brick gatehouse and the long concrete façade of the old power canal, both brightly tattooed with graffiti. Half hidden in the woods, they appear like remnants of a long lost civilization.

While not isolated, the spot provides ample solitude. The falls' roar is an insulating sound blocking all outside noise. The smooth water continuously rolling over the concrete spillway and plunging to a milky froth below is alluringly hypnotic and helps focus the mind. It takes but a moment to feel remote despite people nearby.

I'm energized at this oasis of tranquillity. Long out of business, the axe and machete manufacturing Collins Company recognized the river's power early in the last century when it built the dam to funnel water 650 feet downstream to a powerhouse that spun twin turbines generating a combined 700 horsepower. Now, with the water unbridled by any dynamo, I can contemplate that unfettered power and let it flow through me. At the same time I share the river's force, it has a calming influence. Any restiveness or agitation easily flows downstream.

As water tumbles over the precipice and I feel its mild thunder in my chest, I often concentrate on breathing, feel my abdomen rise and fall, the chest expand and contract. The mind gains free reign and wanders like a dog out for a walk.

At this one time site of industrial power I now enjoy a place rich in natural beauty and deep ecological function where I feel the kinetic energy of moving water while gazing at the slowly deteriorating imprint of humanity. I've spent many hours here wondering about our need for a deeper mutual relationship with the natural world. Thought fragments and fleeting ideas have come to me while almost in a listening-point-dream-state. Over the years, I've pieced together a framework that helps explain, to me at least, where that relationship with nature has been and where it might be going.

"In wildness is the preservation of the world," Henry D. Thoreau uttered in one of his lightning-bolt aphorisms. The earth's wild places have clearly shrunk since his time, making the remaining ones even more precious for the homeostatic regulation of the planet. But beyond ecological value, their worth as wellsprings of human imagination have grown exponentially as their acreage has contracted. Counter intuitively, perhaps, protection of such places requires we appreciate nearby landscapes. To turn the Concord naturalist's dictum somewhat around, I'm convinced that in built spaces where we live is the preservation of the wild. Terranexus is necessary for human survival. I've heard this mantra whispered in the wind and falling water at my listening point.

41

II. CONSERVATION'S FOURTH WAVE

America has experienced three waves of conservation consciousness pointing the way to *terranexus.*

While scientists, politicians, and artists, sportsmen and travelers have contributed to each wave, writers have probably been the most influential. No wonder Bill McKibben, one of today's finest environmental authors, has observed that "an argument can be made that environmental writing is America's single most distinctive contribution to the world's literature."

The first wave established an awareness of the beauty and diversity of nature, creating a realization that the natural world was not just something for exploitation. While there are antecedents, in America this approach was pioneered by Thoreau whose masterpiece, Walden, was published in 1854. The book is full of keen nature observations and acerbic critiques of society, but most significantly makes a compelling connection between human consciousness and natural objects and phenomena, the first stirrings of terranexus. To some extent, all environmental writing is a footnote to Thoreau, but there are many clear-eyed and compelling authors in this first-wave tradition of awareness. These include Catskill naturalist John Burroughs in the later nineteenth century, and Edwin Way Teale who won the Pulitzer Prize for one of his epic four volumes about seasonal change in the twentieth. Among contemporary writers are John Hanson Mitchell who interweaves human culture with nature, and time with place. Another is Robert Finch, whose Cape Cod essays tie personal experience with history and nature's cycles.

The second wave launched from the first. It called not just for awareness and appreciation, but activism to protect beauty, ecological functions and other values. Mountain wanderer and Sierra Club founder John Muir is the progenitor, advocating for creation of national parks and in defense of forests. His poetic pleas to save Hetch Hetchy Valley and the redwoods remain moving, an expression of terranexus through efforts to protect places. This approach has included late twentieth and early twenty-first century authors as diverse as eco-anarchist Edward Abbey and climate change activist McKibben. Perhaps this second wave of conservation consciousness reached its zenith with Rachel Carson's Silent Spring, the 1962 blockbuster about the toxic dangers of pesticides that launched modern environmentalism and enabled us to clearly see the connection between human activity and the health of our landscape.

A third wave that introduced ethical conservation consciousness began with forester and ecologist Aldo Leopold, most well known for A Sand County Almanac. His land ethic "changes the role of Homo sapiens from conqueror of the land community to plain member and citizen of it," advancing terranexus via both a practical and moral connection of people to places. Integral to that view is an ecological way of thinking. "Land, then," he wrote, "is not merely soil; it is a fountain of energy flowing through a circuit of soils, plants and animals." Though once termed a "subversive science," an ecological worldview is today widely accepted though, unfortunately, less well practiced. Its best contemporary expression is in the writings of Kentuckian Wendell Berry who knows "Nature is party to all our deals and decisions, and she has more votes, a longer memory, and a sterner sense of justice than we do." The same sense of ecological connection flashes through the works of essayists Scott Russell Sanders and Annie Dillard. In fact, there is some element of Leopold's enviro-ethics in all the best writers that have come after him.

Leopold's land ethic imbued with terranexus could herald a fourth wave of conservation consciousness, encouraging us to prize not just pristine and magnificent places—the Yellowstones of the world—but more mundane precincts. A sense of terranexus encourages us to consciously explore rather than sleepwalk through areas where we live, work and visit. Exploration entices us to learn more, and as we come to know such places better we increasingly learn to appreciate them, hopefully even come to love them. And to the extent we appreciate and love them, we'll recognize our connection and want to invest our time, energy and money to protect and make them better. As we come to value familiar places, distant wonders will only grow in our esteem.

Garnering inspiration from mundane places to protect singular ones may sound far-fetched, but it is exactly in the Leopold mode. Though Leopold worked and lived in some of the American West's most fabulous country, it was a patch of worn-out land in an ordinary Wisconsin sand county on which he most lavished his love and found inspiration for world changing ideas. Leopold explained that "the [human] individual is a member of a community of interdependent parts." Likewise, terranexus erases, or at least blurs the lines between human and wild communities, between the built and natural environments, recognizing

their linked ecology because "man is, in fact, only a member of a biotic team."

If ecological science teaches one basic lesson everyone readily understands, it's that all things are connected. But the connections we perceive at the scale of a wolf's territory or the habitat of bog turtles, a skunk cabbage filled wetland, and even at a watershed level, tend to be forgotten with regard to humanity, whether in rural areas, suburbs or large cities. Even among those who have elevated Leopold to near-sainthood, there seems some amnesia over the fact that he first explained natural communities by reference to their human analog, places where man's "instincts prompt him to compete for his place in that community, but his ethics prompt him also to co-operate."

Despite notable exceptions, the world seems to be divided into those who enjoy the pulse of urbanity and those who seek the flow of nature, those who often find the built environment too frenetic and ugly, and those for whom the natural world is dull and frightening. It is a chasm at least as wide as that perceived between science and the humanities in C.P. Snow's famous 1959 lecture, "The Two Cultures." Perhaps we need a deeper, more ecological way of looking at the world requiring slower, more deliberate movement through the landscape than we commonly experience. Sometimes we need simply to walk.

Many great conservationists have been inveterate walkers. After all, afoot is often the best means of traveling in wilder places. Inasmuch as what we perceive is often inversely proportional to how fast we move, going slowly enables us to see and understand more, essential conditions for terranexus. Furthermore, walking is a great stimulant to thought. "The rhythm of walking generates a kind of rhythm of thinking, and the passage through a landscape echoes or stimulates the passage through a series of thoughts," writes Rebecca Solnit in Wanderlust.

It comes as no surprise that Thoreau, Muir, and Teale are among many famous walkers who have shaped our understanding and love of nature. But the same is true of many great thinkers and lovers of urban areas such as twentieth century social critic Lewis Mumford who won the 1962 National Book Award for The City in History, or Alfred Kazin, a literary critic of the same era whose A Walker in the City fuses personal experience with acute observation of architecture and the human ecology of neighborhoods. Among contemporary writers, Harvard's John Stilgoe continues to explore city and suburb by foot and bicycle.

Terranexus teaches that built places can be just as beautiful, intriguing and curious as natural marvels. And a mix of the two often provides the most fascinating environments. Perhaps this is why my sense of terranexus first emerged in the White Mountains where both nature and human works stun the senses. Nature is awe inspiring, but the huts, well engineered trails, and features like the Mount Washington Cog Railway are critical to the experience.

City walkers are in the grand European tradition of the flaneur, the somewhat aimless wanderers who know urban areas with their raw senses, by footstep. Careful observers like naturalists, they distill stories from the architectural features of buildings whether it be a brick bond pattern, plate glass, or neon sign. They know how sunlight and shadow play on a plaza at various times of day and changes with the seasons. When a street is dug up they notice remnants of barrel stave water mains and cobblestone pavement. To a flaneur the past is always present. They know the stories of former inhabitants and watch the habits and moods of people in shops, on the street, and in cafes.

Nature and the world of human structures are inextricably linked. It's not civilization that is artificial or unnatural, but the distinction we have drawn between them. We need to extend hiking trails through cities, connecting them to wilder precincts. I'd like to see the blazes that take us up mountains and along bucolic waterbodies also mark paths through urban areas as does Boston's Freedom Trail. The New England Trail, newest of the eleven national scenic trails established by Congress does just that on its way from Long Island Sound toward New Hampshire's Mount Monadnock. Starting in Guilford, Connecticut, the first few miles take hikers past a veritable timeline of buildings representing almost 400 years of European settlement, including New England's oldest stone house.

The synergies of nature and culture first struck me while walking Boston's Emerald Necklace, a ten mile long series of connected green spaces that snake along the city's backbone from the historic Common to Franklin Park. A few years before paddling the Naugatuck, I discovered the route by accident when opening a crease-worn map to direct a friend to a Red Sox game. For the first time, I noticed swatches of deep green in the grid of city streets.

Much of the Necklace and the concept of making connections among city greenspaces was

the brainchild of Frederick Law Olmsted, father of American landscape architecture, who is most famous for designing New York's Central Park. The route became my portal to discovering a rich mixture of history, art, architecture, birdlife, open waters and forest. But it wasn't all bucolic beauty. I also found pollution, invasive species, graffiti, a man urinating in the bushes, and broken walkways and bridges.

Each park along the necklace was a jewel commemorating a different aspect of Boston. With its walkways and tree shaded lawns the Common memorializes famous people and events with statuary and plaques. These objects commemorating the past were like tangible shadows in a place busy with tourists, concerts, and ballgames. From the Common, I entered the well planted flower beds and carefully groomed grass of the Public Garden which exuded a traditional Bostonian atmosphere of restrained formality. On the Commonwealth Avenue Mall, a wide linear swath of green dividing lanes of traffic, tree colonnades formed a leafy tunnel between low cliffs of brownstone and brick row houses lining the street.

Walking through the linear Backbay Fens and Riverway I passed bodies of water that were once tidal marshes and then fetid dumps for sewage. Today, Olmsted's green spaces are interrupted by roads, and parts of them are given over to athletic fields, community gardens and other uses. Nevertheless, I saw painted and snapping turtles basking in the sun, green and bull frogs hunched at the water's edge, and lots of birds from kingfishers to black crowned night herons, black ducks, mallards, and Canada geese. Children fished for carp, and held their catches high for me to see. Of course there was the inevitable half drowned shopping cart, some beer and soda bottles and other detritus in the water. Somewhere in this mixture of nature and trash the hopes and regrets of urban life seemed unwittingly expressed.

The Emerald Necklace continued to the open

horizons and beautifully reflective waters of Jamaica Pond, a former reservoir, and then to the Arnold Arboretum, a place of both natural beauty and scientifically planted trees from every temperate region of the globe. I finally arrived at Franklin Park whose connection to the rest of the Necklace is tenuous because an Olmsted proposed parkway was never built. Large for a city park, its over 400 acres contained seemingly wild forests dense with maple, oak, and beech. But there were also invasive plants common in developed areas, like barberry and Japanese knotweed. There's a meadow disguised as a golf course, and a zoo. I watched red-tailed hawks wheeling overhead and wandered through places where not a single building was visible.

The Emerald Necklace is no wilderness, but perhaps it has sufficient wildness, as Thoreau would have it, to help preserve the world. Although nature purists might emphasize limitations, I felt exhilaration in finding nature and culture so well married. In Boston, an urban dweller does not have to flee the city to walk slightly on the wild side. If a traditional urban environment had these places, I wondered about the possibilities in less thickly settled areas. It seemed that preserving and promoting such nodes of wildness close to where people live could both enrich daily existence and save truly wild areas for special visits, thus avoiding their overuse. We need to be naturalists of urbanity, flaneurs of the wild.

In an age where preserved natural places like the White Mountains and Great Smoky Mountains National Park are often shrouded in air pollution and eaten alive by invasive species that come in the wake of human commerce, treating cities and wild places as distinct, unrelated islands seems particularly puzzling. How many people realize that the location of cities, housing tracts, agricultural fields, factories, and even the contour of roads are often largely dictated by bedrock and glacial geology and other natural factors? And recent books like David Owen's *Green Metropolis* and Edward Glaeser's *Triumph of the City* make a compelling case that if you care about nature, city living is preferred because urban dwellers require less living space, use less fuel, produce less trash and spend fewer hours in cars. Spreading people thinly across the countryside, Owen writes, "may make them feel greener, but … increases the damage, while also making the problems they cause harder to see and address."

Perhaps the link between built and natural environments was most elegiacally captured by journalist Howard Mansfield in his book The Same Ax, Twice. "The house is more like a natural landscape," he writes. "You are looking at time. Seven generations of life represented by a notch on a girt, a paint chip on a summer beam, the way the head of an adze met the wood one winter day in 1664. Life flowed through here and like a glacier left its marks upon wood and plaster." Such connections are the very soul of terranexus.

III. WOUNDED PLACES

For many of us, our appreciation of landscapes and an impulse toward terranexus is most intense where nature is dominant, from mountains to beaches, black spruce bogs to floodplain forests.

They seduce us with their distinct beauty and refreshing differences from our usual haunts. But to be fully aware of and appreciate this world, our attachment must extend to working landscapes of farm and forest which provide food and fiber and offer a rich patchwork of trees, pasture, and cropland. It must embrace historic colonial towns with their broad greens, and nineteenth-century mill villages with their fortress-like factories. It needs to include city neighborhoods, commercial and industrial districts, both those that are well maintained and those suffering neglect. All these places help explain who we are as a

society and as individuals. To see only those that please us is to inhabit a Disneyland of our own making.

While they need no encouragement or protection, even strip developments with their garish signs, confusing traffic lanes, fast food restaurants, filling stations and big box stores are functional parts of our landscape along with interstate highways and housing tracts. We may think some of these landscapes ugly and wasteful, but few of us do not use them. And I admit to feeling an occasional thrum of excitement in the busy commerce of a strip mall, or the cinematic movement of topography at sixty-five miles per hour. All these are areas in which we live, work and do business. They are places that deserve our interest and attention. The more we understand them, the more we will know what is needed to create better places.

Regardless of our attempts to minimize and see some value in less than ideal places, there will always be landscapes severely compromised in support of a civilization that also builds meaningful cultural spaces and protects the beauty of nature. Places sacrificed for the less glorious needs of civilization include those chosen for waste disposal, energy development, mineral extraction, and other uses that severely damage the land. I'm reminded of F. Scott Fitzgerald's "valley of ashes" in *The Great Gatsby*, a "desolate area" of "gray land" with "spasms of bleak dust which drift endlessly over it."

After shrinking the need for them as much as feasible, do we justify such places as necessary evils supporting a greater good? Do we try seeing a stark beauty in their barren and often toxic precincts? Sometimes poisoned places, of which Chernobyl is the supreme example, become accidental wildernesses, opportunities for a revival of nature, though at great human cost and unknown long term impacts to the plant and animal communities that recolonize them.

Ultimately, we must acknowledge our culpability in devastating some parts of the planet. Perhaps the best we can do is maintain consciousness of their pernicious impacts and hope such awareness motivates us to limit these zones. "Certainly these sad, toxic, taboo places deserve as much recognition and gratitude as their unmolested counterparts," Trebe Johnson argued in a 2015 issue of Orion magazine, about a slice of bucolic Pennsylvania sacrificed for hydrofracking. "By offering a bit of beauty," she writes, "to a being or place that has been felled, fracked, polluted, abused, or in some other way robbed of its dignity and purpose, I can replenish its loveliness. By believing—and then acting on—the conviction that a place is worthy of receiving some kind of gift, my consciousness shifts from anger, disgust, or sadness to one of compassion, engagement and creativity."

Johnson's notion may seem somewhat romantic, but sometimes there's nothing else we can do. Although such places are not usually sources of creative inspiration, perhaps some of that loveliness can be replenished with art. Robert Smithson, most famous for monumental land art like his 1,500-foot-long Spiral Jetty extending into Utah's Great Salt Lake, chastised artists who retreated to scenic beauty spots rather than try to form a dialectic between people and nature. As early as the 1960s he saw the industrial landscapes of northern New Jersey as worthy of artistic expression.

Maybe the best way to express gratitude for the places we have wounded is to repair those that can be healed. This may be a cleaned brownfield put to new economic use or the site of a demolished building that can be reborn as a garden or pocket park. Even landfills can be transformed.

The old Hartford landfill, a mound that rises about 130 feet above the surrounding landscape, is not far from my home and among my favorite degraded places to visit. Sandwiched between Interstate 91 and the Connecticut River in the north end of the city, it accepted garbage and incinerator ash from 1940 to 1988. Now the grassy mound is healing. Wells drilled into the interior have produced methane gas to generate electricity and a solar panel array has been installed. In season, the uneven plateau sports a startlingly lustrous prairie of waist high grass where daisies, lacy yarrow, buttercup, white and red clover, hawkweed, the purplish pea-like blossoms of cow vetch, and many other common roadside flowers bloom profusely. The grasses and sky resound with avian life. When I was last there, redwing blackbirds cruised just above the meadow and uncommon savannah sparrows alighted on fencepost-sized gas wellhead pipes. A spotted sandpiper with a clutch of young crossed the gravel wheel track, and a killdeer scurried away performing a fake broken wing routine. A great blue heron flew overhead with its long legs outstretched and red-tailed hawks circled far above. There was a kingbird, indigo buntings, orchard and Baltimore orioles, grackles, cedar waxwings whose tail-tips looked as if dipped in yellow paint, goldfinches and other birds. It was a giddy carnival of color and song.

A tour bus operator recently expressed interest in excursions to the landfill's summit for what may be the finest panorama along the banks of New England's longest river. To the north and south, the grand corridor of the Connecticut valley spreads out like a map with trees, fields, water, roadways, church spires, smokestacks, bridges, rooftops, and all the tackle and infrastructure of modern life visible for miles. To the west and east the horizon rises to lumpy, rugged highlands punctuated by a few antennae and towers.

Once a smelly eyesore, this accidental high meadow is becoming a place of intriguing beauty, source of energy, and reserve of biodiversity. Bird expert Jay Kaplan calls it the best grassland habitat in the region. Here is recycling writ large, a debauched and degraded landscape transformed and healing into something else, a spot with a second chance.

It's not possible to restore the swale where Hartford's old landfill now rises, but we might not want to do so even if we could. New opportunities abound for this and other mounds of used up and broken stuff. Less than an hour's drive away, the old Milford landfill—rising fifty feet above the beach at Silver Sands State Park—offers spectacular views of Charles Island and Long Island Sound. When finally developed, visitors will be able to hike or drive cars via a narrow roadway that will spiral around the landform to a summit featuring a pavilion for picnics and weddings. Old landfills have been recast as athletic fields, parking lots and even commercial building spaces. These places may be ugly on the inside, but can be made to look beautiful and become meaningful. We cannot afford to forget their existence or our connection to them.

Landfills are only one among many wounded places that we should remember. While rivers like the Naugatuck have been reborn after dying the death of a thousand polluting discharges, others have been buried because they flooded or pollution made them disgusting. Sometimes they used space that myopic developers and politicians found more suitable for roads and buildings. These rivers may be gone, but not always forgotten. Providence, Rhode Island exposed and moved about two-thirds of a mile of river in the heart of downtown in the 1990s, watercourses that had been sealed for decades beneath roadways and parking areas. The rivers have become an economic driver and tourists flock to walk the tree lined cobblestone paths alongside them, cross the graceful Venetian bridges, take boat rides, and see the world famous WaterFire display with its 86 burning braziers. Experiencing terranexus, caring people connected with Providence's waterways and helped create the city's amazing revival.

Terranexus demands we declare war on the kind of cultural dementia that causes us to ignore such places. True lovers of landscape see not only today's prospect, but imagine what once was and what might yet be. They make the places where we dwell more livable. We must explore forgotten and forbidding places so we can tell their stories. Such places beckon with unexpected adventure.

Like Providence, Hartford also has a buried watercourse. The Park River is invisible in the last two miles before its confluence with the Connecticut River. Its waters are never pelted by raindrops, ruffled by wind or dappled with sunlight. Most people are unaware a river runs through the city because it runs beneath it. The Park was buried by the Army Corps of Engineers between the 1930s and 1980s, punished by entombment in massive concrete conduits for the sin of destructive floods caused by poor development in its watershed.

For years I passed the twenty-seven-foot-high tunnel opening on my way to work. At last curiosity about its course got the best of me. Although in high water the trip could be extremely dangerous, I found that low water offered a peculiar paddle through an ersatz wilderness devoid of people, roads, buildings, sun, and sky. It was an eerie, dank world of echoes and eternal night that enfeebled even the brightest flashlight.

Colorful graffiti marked the entrance, but light quickly faded until reverberating sounds and a swampy smell dominated the senses. Riffles around occasional rocks and a little water seeping from above were as loud as waterfalls. Glancing around with a headlamp I saw smooth masonry walls punctuated with metal capped sluice gates and screened intakes. Although the darkness was daunting, the trip was remarkably uneventful. No filth floated on the water; there were no clots of garbage or unexpected rapids. Only a small school of catfish clustering around the boat near the tunnel's end was noteworthy. Ultimately, I emerged from the disquiet and constriction of darkness into an eye-squinting explosion of light and space on the Connecticut River, the city's skyline behind me.

This river may never become a favorite paddle of canoeists. But the underground experience holds a bizarre allure that mixes our fascination with oversized engineering feats, fear of darkness, attraction to moving water and desire for offbeat experiences. A local outfitter was once interested in leading commercial trips, but city bureaucrats and risk managers axed that idea. Thus, the Park River remains an outlaw journey, perhaps amping its allure. It may be out of sight, but should never be out of mind. This forever dark reach of river has much to teach about the ultimate price we pay for abusing our waterways, about engineering, development, public works, and history.

IV DEEP TRAVELING

How can we experience teranexus and narrow the divide between wild and built landscapes?

How will teranexus revive interest in the conservation of unique natural and cultural places? Only by deep travel, a form of practiced, concentrated observation amplifying what we see close to home.

The commonplace world around us brims with stories that deep travelers detect, whether they are found in the distant geological record of bedrock displayed at roadside rock cuts, at cemeteries, or in street names. Our landscape is dotted with revealing clues that enable us to read what has happened and what might be. Deep travelers know this and see the world in high definition.

Deep travelers go beyond what is visible and unlock the stories hidden in people, places and phenomena. They see connections and narratives everywhere. Deep travelers connect the dots among diverse phenomena such as swift streams, nineteenth century waterpower factories with worker housing, and twenty-first century neighborhood ethnicities. A deep traveler perceives changes over time, observes history in roadside milestones, building materials, abandoned structures, and the tales people tell on the street, in coffee shops and barrooms. It's not merely a matter of improved visual acuity, but transfigured vision that injects awe and wonder into everyday experience. Deep traveling leads to intimate place knowledge. Knowledge begets understanding, and understanding leads to teranexus, profound connection to places both singular and ordinary.

Traveling deeply requires no mystical sixth sense or specialized academic training, only sensitivity to the simple language of the landscape. The words are the details we see every day, from big trees to swayback barns. The grammar is found in the way we weave those isolated details into sentences and paragraphs of meaning that create narratives. No artifact, whether a stone wall or a housing tract, is an isolated word or sentence in the story of people and landscape.

People who care about places must be deep travelers. We are obligated to tell stories that will excite those blind and deaf to the everyday magic animating both ordinary and unique areas. No place, not a polluted wasteland nor a seemingly boring subdivision is without compelling tales and fascinating human and landscape confluences. Those who cannot see these links need to look harder or differently. We must be cartographers of imagination, drawing what unconventional travel writer William Least Heat-Moon calls a "deep map," an amalgam of topography, history, biography, folklore, politics, geology and natural history.

Deep travel heightens awareness, creates a landscape consciousness that results in terranexus. Such purposeful looking is more than a windshield tour or a plat-like view from a plane. It is often unplanned, serendipitous exploration. "Ordinary exploration begins in casual indirection," writes John Stilgoe in Outside Lies Magic, "in the juiciest sort of indecision, in deliberate, then routine fits of absence of mind. Walk three quarters of the way around the block, then strike out on a vector, a more or less straight line toward nothing in particular, follow the downgrade or the newer pavement, head for the shadow of trees ahead, strike off toward the sound of the belfry clock, follow the scent of the bakery back door, drift downhill toward the river."

Opportunities for deep travel exploring exist all around us and only await our imaginations to match the rich complexity of the landscape. Few realize, for instance, that cemeteries are as much for the living as for the dead. Beyond being places to pay respects to our predecessors, graveyards are schoolrooms of history, sculpture, genealogy and natural history. They play host to endangered species, and are often ideal places to observe birds, wildflowers, mushrooms, butterflies and other natural delights.

In old industrial precincts we sometimes find power and transportation canals that take us to the very intersection of nature and invention. They can be repurposed for boating, fishing and the sheer enjoyment of walking beside their waters. Lowell National Historical Park in Massachusetts, a cradle of American textile production, has long made use of these artificial rivers for the education and sheer enjoyment of the public.

Abandoned railroad rights-of-way repurposed for non-motorized travel, like the one that leads to my listening point, increasingly take us to experience nature, even in the heart of urban areas. The elevated railway known as the High Line on Manhattan's west side, built for industrial freight, has been reengineered into a walkway above city streets. Now filled with naturalistic plantings and birdsong, it offers spacious views of the sky and horizon, pleasures that are sometimes at a premium amidst city towers. Striding along the route is energizing. Simultaneously I feel the galvanizing movement of the city and the soothing elements of nature.

Deep travelers know that ruins can add drama, beauty, and meaning to our landscape. Tumbledown structures like mills, grand houses, and public buildings are not necessarily eyesores or signs of blight. Properly curated, they are opportunities to enrich our culture and provide economic development. They can instill community pride and prepare us for future change by illustrating time's passage.

Nineteenth century painters like Thomas Cole and writers like Washington Irving lamented that this nation lacked ruins to chronicle the past and give depth to its countryside. Though the most famous of Hudson River School painters is best remembered for canvasses depicting the grandeur of America's natural scenery, Frederic Church traveled to Greece, the middle east and elsewhere to capture the moldering remains of old buildings. Today this deep traveling genius of American art could have stayed home and painted abandoned factories, some of which stand like noble castles along our waterways.

Not every crumbling mill and other structures ought to be saved as ruins, but it's time we realize that restoration and demolition aren't the sole alternatives. Those who think stabilized ruins don't add pecuniary value should talk to British tourism officials about Roman remnants and the remains of abbeys and towers. Closer to home, the Eastern States Penitentiary in Philadelphia is a preserved ruin attracting thousands annually, as are the brick remnants of a Barboursville, Virginia house designed by Thomas Jefferson, and the cliff dwellings of Colorado's Mesa Verde National Park.

Architectural ruins demonstrate nature's relentlessness as a solvent of all humankind creates. They evidence our constant battle against the forces of entropy. Not every example of picturesque decay is worthy, but we will be remiss if we fail to make an effort to protect and interpret those that can enliven our landscape by visibly and tangibly telling a story of ingenuity, hard work, and other transcendent values.

Renewed enthusiasm for natural and cultural resource conservation depends on deep travelers, people of insight who care about places near and far, to light fires of enthusiasm under those around them. We can talk about the magnificence of distant regions, but we will be most effective if we start generating more interest in familiar spots, like Leopold did for his beloved patch of tired sand county. The first step is to steep ourselves in the natural and cultural history, science, legends, and lore of the everyday areas where we live, work and play. We must tell stories that give meaning to those places. This is the essence of deep travel, the heart of terranexus.

The need for balanced, diverse, healthy functioning systems transcends differences between built and natural worlds. Most times we experience synergies between the two. "What we long for," wrote the eminent biologist Rene Dubois, "is rarely nature in the raw, more often it is a landscape suited to human limitations and shared by the efforts and aspirations that have created civilized life." Paradoxically, revival of the conservation movement and protection of our most magnificent places lies in understanding and appreciating those areas where natural values are not necessarily pure or ascendant. It's not just a matter of demonstrating that the economy and culture of cities are codependent on the complexities of natural habitats, but of valuing a relationship regardless of similarities and distinctions. A sane, sustainable future demands ecological thinking in the built environment and understanding of how culture affects the natural world. It demands better connection to the everyday landscapes around us. It demands terranexus.

When in the woods we need to extol old mill dams, faded roads, farm walls, abandoned quarries, changing plant assemblages, and rock outcrops that illuminate the "why" of a place. Here in New England, for example, we must relate the story of primeval forest, Native habitation, colonial farming, early industry, reforestation, and development. While walking in our neighborhoods, we must be attuned to architecture that speaks of fashion, money, and technology as we recall quirky residents and past land uses. Street names alone often read like a completed crossword puzzle inviting us to pose the questions that they answer. We must make places personal by conveying that such stories are also our story, that we exist in the very continuum we describe. Richer places mean richer lives. The places where we live can be places that we love if we dare to make the investment—not of money, but of time and energy.

The deepest travel begins at home. Splendor awaits just beyond the doorstep.

DAVID K. LEFF (HE/HIM) is an award-winning poet and essayist, and former deputy commissioner of the Connecticut Department of Environmental Protection. He is the Canton, Connecticut poet laureate, deputy town historian, and town meeting moderator. He was a volunteer firefighter for 26 years. In 2016 and 2017 David was appointed to serve as poet-in-residence for the New England National Scenic Trail (NET). He has been nominated three times for a Pushcart Prize, and has twice been a finalist in the Connecticut Book Awards. David has received two silver medals from the Independent Publisher Book Awards (IPPY), and was grand prize short-listed for the Eric Hoffer Book Award. His work has appeared in anthologies, newspapers such as the *Hartford Courant*, and magazines including Appalachia and Yankee. The author of seven nonfiction books, three volumes of poetry, and two novels in verse, David's work focuses on the connection of people to their communities and the natural environment. He often explores commonplace elements of the world around us that have hidden meanings and unusual links to each other. David has been the book review editor of *Connecticut Woodlands*, the quarterly magazine of the *Connecticut Forest & Park Association* and is now poetry editor. He is a Senior Editor for *Wayfarer Magazine*. View his work at www.davidkleff.com

WHAT COMES NEXT

BETWEEN BEAUTY AND DESTRUCTION

AN ESSAY BY HEIDI BARR

This is the story of the time I lost my job.

The story starts well before my last day with an employer of ten years, and it continues well after starting something new. It even continues after the last page you'll turn in this book. Because the days continue to churn on, and many of them are just like any other ordinary day. But, as it turns out, all of these ordinary days, when strung together make up part of a human life. A life that is full of meaning, uncertainty, and the beautiful contrast that comes with being alive on the earth at this time in history. What comes next? None of us can ever know. We can only live the moments, from those full of beauty to those defined by destruction, as they unfold.

October means it's peak autumn color in Minnesota once again, and everywhere you look, it's gorgeous. The leaves in the back of my house blaze yellow and orange, and they create an impressive reflection on the lake when the light is just so and the air is still. It's kind of like the water is on fire with the vibrancy of the season. Of course, this time of intense beauty is fleeting, only lasting a few weeks each year, but then again, it does come back around every year. I just have to make a point to pay attention to it when it does show up. It's always interesting to me that such intense beauty can co-exist so easily alongside the things that shake us to the core.

October 19th I walked into my home office after a fabulous morning hiking with my young daughter, ready for a few hours of work before joining her and my spouse in the afternoon for more outside play time. Just as I was getting ready to dial into the weekly staff meeting, my phone rang, and I answered it since I saw it was my supervisor.

"Hello, this is Heidi. How's your day?" I said, as that was my usual greeting.

"Hello, Heidi. Thanks for taking this call today. We regret to inform you that as of December 2nd, your position is being eliminated."

Late autumn marks the time of year I got the news that I was being laid off from my job of ten years. While this unexpected turn of events was certainly not a tragedy of the magnitude of trying to remake life in the aftermath of a hurricane or managing a chronic disease or seeing your home go up in flames or losing a child to violence, there have been some studies that show that when people lose a job, it leaves an impact as significant as losing a spouse. I'm not sure I totally buy that, despite what the statistics say, but I can see the parallels. We assign so much meaning to our work, it can feel like our identity and self-worth are stripped away when that job is lost. It feels like I should have been able to prevent it somehow. It invites feelings of inadequacy. And, let's

be honest, having a corporate paycheck and the benefits package that comes with it makes a difference in how easy life feels, especially when the job that goes away is the one that had been the primary support of a family for a long time.

Every time this season of beauty comes around again, I find myself reflecting on the things I've learned as a result of what came to pass that autumn that I heard the news that I was being laid off.

I wouldn't change what happened. Sounds odd, but I don't know if I would have had the courage to leave when left to my own devices. I was burnt out and every day was stressful. I would have, of course, preferred to leave on my own terms with a heartfelt goodbye and the typical "thanks for all of your service, we wish you well" email that was the typical protocol when an employee resigned by their own choice, (because who wouldn't?) but I am owning up to the fact that I hadn't figured out how to do that without the extra push.

The first Monday after the last day at a job you've held for nearly ten years is a strange day.

I spent it making scones with my daughter in the morning after running in the frosty sunlight on the gravel roads of the neighborhood. My little family and I got ready for the day, and then my spouse Nick and our daughter Eva left for an appointment in the city. At about the time that I had always started the workday in my home office, I loaded my work computer into the Jeep, spent a few too many minutes wasting time on social media, and eventually made my way to the closest FedEx ship spot. Two trips back and forth to the car, plus ten dollars and twenty minutes later, I was done. Aside from one more paycheck and collecting a modest severance package, my title as a corporate health coach was a thing of the past.

I didn't really know what to think about it that day—I was rather tired of thinking about the transition since it had been on my mind since I got the news of the layoff six weeks before. After saying farewell to the computer, I drove home and cleaned out the office that had hosted my work for so many years. I thought about burning some sage to cleanse the space of negative energy, and though I never actually got around to doing that, I did light some old paperwork on fire and created a small altar: a rock that I picked up in Malta 20 years ago, a feather, a little statue of a person holding their hands to the sky. I added a yoga mat, some more house plants and told myself this was just another opportunity to deepen my practice and get clear on what I wanted to do next. Some days I even believed myself.

I have always worked in healthcare. The job I lost was that of "corporate health coach." So perhaps that's a good place to start, with a glimpse into the industry of "health" —because all stories need a foundation.

When you work in the healthcare field, whether it's in a fitness center, in customer service, in management, in coaching (as I have), as a physician, as a nurse, or as an administrative assistant, you are reminded on a regular basis that life is hard for people. People are stressed out, people are managing chronic conditions, people have financial issues, people are grieving, people are angry, people are unsure. People are also happy, satisfied, healthy, and thriving, but folks tend to share their struggles before they share their joys. Interacting with humanity, especially when it comes to something as intimate as one's health and wellbeing, is messy and unpredictable no matter how hard we try to make it into a program, sell a product, round out the edges, or meet our outcomes goals. So often we, myself included, have the urge to swoop in to offer a solution, to look at the numbers and provide a suggestion, or to give advice based on what we see or hear. There is nothing wrong with doing these things, and often times, doing these things is good and necessary. But the other side is that we miss something when we don't allow space for witnessing what needs to be witnessed and providing support in a way that can't be measured.

As Parker Palmer writes, "The human [soul] doesn't want to be advised or fixed or saved. It simply wants to be witnessed—to be seen, heard and companioned exactly as it is. When we make that kind of deep bow to the soul of a suffering person, our respect reinforces the soul's healing resources, the only resources that can help the sufferer make it through."

One of our best offerings to other humans, no matter what our vocation but especially in healthcare, is the gift of presence, of listening, and of showing up in a way that is authentic. When I can get past my own fear of being uncomfortable with hard situations and to the place where I can give someone a period of real connection, I offer those with whom I interact something that is more valuable than any piece of advice could ever be. Poet Mary Oliver writes, "This is the first, the wildest and the wisest thing I know: that the soul exists and is built entirely out of attentiveness."

When I can get to that place of attentiveness, I can bear witness to what is going on, even on the toughest of days, and in doing so acknowledge and honor the deep parts of what being human on this earth is all about. Despite the broken pieces of our conventional healthcare systems, at the core, healthcare is about cultivating wholeness.

*

On that first Monday after my last day, I had plenty of time to think. After all, when you don't have a job, the one thing you do have is time. Even as I grieved losing the security that came from steady employment, I was afraid of getting another corporate job. The lifestyle we'd been living, though modest, was built on a corporate paycheck. We needed a certain amount of cash flow to maintain the house and pay the bills, and the job that had just ended was the foundation of our income. But I didn't want to put our daughter into daycare just so I could work a job that didn't matter to me. I didn't want to sell out at that point in my life, knowing what I knew about our culture and the demons that ride on the shoulders of money. I was afraid of becoming one of the cliches that I have been so against for years: a person who commutes for three hours every single day to work a job they hate just to pay the mortgage of a house they never spend time in. Becoming that person was not something I was interested in doing, no matter what the rate of pay.

I felt foolish for putting all of my eggs in one work basket. We moved to the country, about an hour's drive from the nearest metro area, and bought our house that sits on an small acreage because I was able to work from home. My reviews at work were always good, I had one of the longest tenures of the department, and job security was a thing that other people had to worry about.

Two and a half years before that first Monday after I lost my job.

Spring

My day job is to support people as they figure out how to live in a healthy way. I've been in my current position for nearly seven years, and though I truly value the relationships that I have with the people I interact with and can see the reason for most of the less glamorous job tasks that are required, last week I hit a bit of a wall. And when I say "hit a wall" I mean in a head-on collision, can't function kind of way. I just couldn't do it anymore. So I spent the two days I took off work sleeping, getting a haircut that was two years overdue, walking along my favorite creek bed and doing yoga. I feel better after four days away from the office, but it's not gone yet.

What causes burnout? Long hours, a job that is too challenging or not challenging enough, monotony, a long winter, a disconnect between employer and employee values, being in a caregiver role, always being the one to ask "how are you today?" and responding appropriately to whatever response is provided......the list could get pretty long. Whatever the root cause, burnout can have a lot of impact on day to day life. According to psychologist Herbert J. Freudenberger, who coined the term in 1972, burnout is a "state of fatigue or frustration brought about by devotion to a cause, a way of life, or a relationship that has failed to produce the expected reward. Burnout is essentially a condition caused by passion and good intentions that have absorbed everything that is available to give."

My next step is going to be figuring out how to take some more time off. We'll see how that goes. The good news is that my light is flickering on again, even if it's dim.

Even when it's dim, I can remember why I have been so devoted, and I can remember that to be devoted—to anything—I have to take care of my own needs.

For me, some of the important things to prioritize are spending time with my family, having authentic conversations with people, being outside, growing and cooking food, hearing my daughter giggle, digging in the garden and watching the sunrise. When I can remember that those things are what matter to me, (which can be REALLY hard to do when feelings of burnout have clouded everything else) I can break through the film of melancholy. I can see past the frustration, fatigue and dread of the everyday. And I can remember that I have a choice to let those feelings control my life, or I can look at them, accept them, and allow them to dissolve in whatever way they need to.

Burnout isn't a nice place to be. But it doesn't have to be my landing place. But wow. There have been weeks when I've just kept landing there. There have been so many days when I would have preferred to throw my phone, outlook calendar and headset into the lake.

One of the reasons for my continual visitation to the land of burnout stems from the fact that part of my day job is calling people to schedule coaching appointments. Usually people are polite and respectful, and some are even downright kind-hearted and pleasant to talk to. Which is good news, since the purpose of my calling is to put them on my own coaching calendar, so we'll be talking again. It is helpful to start the relationship off on a positive note.

But one day I called a gentleman who wasn't any of those things. Quite the opposite, really, he was quite mean and disrespectful. I asked if he wanted to set up an appointment, and he responded with sentences

that tended to start with "you people" and "do you even realize" and so on, punctuated by sarcastic chuckling. In short, he made it personal and he wanted me to acknowledge that I was in the wrong. I was the enemy, and he was going to let me know it. Usually I am good at being able to internalize the fact that everyone is dealing with a plethora of issues that I know nothing about and that are quite probably very challenging, resulting in unfriendly behavior; and hey, maybe this man was just having a tough day, or week, or year. His energy was the product of some of the things that are broken in our culture, and at the end of the day, even angry and mean people need love, too. But that day, when he was scolding me for not being able to meet his expectations, all I could hear was "you aren't good enough" and "this is why it's doing me a disservice." I felt like the bad child who doesn't measure up, and I found myself apologizing and trying to hold back tears. Which is really interesting, as I did nothing "wrong" and was quite kind and professional while offering what I had to give. He just didn't find it acceptable. When on the call, I knew intellectually that his issues and his anger were not about me at all, but in the moment his energy triggered a response that I couldn't control. I had to hang up the phone.

A minor part of the day when all was said and done, but something like this hadn't happened at work for a long time, and I like to think that I have developed a thicker skin during my tenure as a corporate health coach. But maybe that's the lesson. Maybe I don't actually want "thick skin." Maybe I want to be able to feel what I feel without having to stifle it to provide good customer service. Maybe I want to be able to offer a service that I know people value, not something that they feel forced to do because of an incentive program through their employer.

I didn't want to talk to him again, yet parts of me said, "This is just another opportunity to grow—working with this person will help you develop better communication and conflict resolution skills." But my gut said, "No. There's absolutely no reason that you should have to interact with that energy again. It's not your job to fix whatever was broken in that interaction."

We can choose, to a point, where to put our energy and where to remove it. There is nothing wrong with placing a boundary between ourselves and something or someone that generates bad energy. It isn't my job to fix everything that crosses my path. No one can always hold space and 'be the light'—it's too much for an individual being to take on. That is not to say that we should close ourselves off to the world and stay cocooned in our own little no-conflict oasis—but it does mean that we should exercise our ability to choose our reality by what we give energy to. It does mean that we should put up boundaries when we need them to stay true to who we are. Maybe in this case it meant to give this gentleman grace, but by way of assigning him a coach with whom he could start off a bit more positively. Sometimes letting go of trying to fix it works better than forcing the desired outcome.

Even though parts of me still said, "Come on, it's not a big thing, just suck it up and deal," another part of me acknowledged the simple fact that instances such as this (one human talking to another human in a way that is not mutually respectful) are commonplace—and, well, that is a big deal. It happens all the time in our world, and that's not okay. It makes me realize that we as a human collective don't need thicker skin. We need more compassion, more love, and more understanding. We need more empathy, more play, and more respect for the other. We need systems that support us, and we need work that matters. We need autonomy and the freedom to choose. We need to honor the boundaries that help us to function at our best. We need to care for ourselves and ensure we aren't compromising our own wellbeing to satisfy someone else.

Dr. Clarissa Pinkola Estes wrote, "There will always be times when you feel discouraged. I too have felt despair many times in my life, but I do not keep a chair for it. I will not entertain it. It is not allowed to eat from my plate." I'm going to follow her lead and not entertain despair over a negative blip in one day that illustrated all that is wrong in the world. Instead, I'm going to remember that the light of the fully lit soul is infinitely more powerful than even the most challenging of interactions and ensure that despair gets not even one crumb.

4 years before
that first Monday
after I lost my job.

Late Summer

Productivity doesn't equal worth. Right? Deep down, I know this statement is absolutely true. At the core, each living being on earth is of infinitely more value than can be measured or quantified. Each person, or creature, or plant, or river is so much more than whatever is accomplished or produced in a lifetime. Yet we as a human collective have a hard time accepting this. We see our land-base as a commodity more often than we see it as a partner in life. We tend to use water and air and soil for our own gain with little thought beyond what our actions might mean for someone across the world or a child born three generations from now. Often we mean well and even start to change our ways, but then life gets hard and it's easier not to. We slip back into believing that more is better and that getting ahead and making the grade is what's important. We start to see high productivity as the ideal and we lose faith in believing that it really isn't when we are trying to tell the truth and the people who have the power to create change don't believe. Or don't want to.

I am trying to be okay with mediocrity.

I've recognized that if I'm going to stay in my day job and thrive as a human being, mediocrity is my new goal for success. It's hard to let old tendencies of wanting to be a top performer or make good grades or always receive glowing reviews go. But I've realized that, at least in my current life and work situation, being a top performer isn't what matters to living the life that I want to live.

I say this, but do I mean it? Can I really be ok with mediocrity and not letting productivity dictate how I feel about my worth in a work setting? What happens when striving for mediocrity is deemed below expectations and unacceptable by the people who decide if you get a paycheck or not? These are hard questions. I can say that I don't care about being called out for not being productive enough, but at the end of the day it still gets under my skin. It still invokes feelings of scarcity and fear of not being enough, no matter how well I do my job. It's challenging to stay true to your convictions when you are told that what you are doing simply isn't good enough to meet corporate goals and that you have to do better, or pay the consequences.

This all sounds more dramatic than it really is, of course. I have an easy life, all things considered. I have a family I love, a beautiful setting to call home, consistent access to good food and water, and a strong and capable body to **see me**

through my days. The stress I have in my life is due to how I perceive what's happening, and I know that I have the capacity to choose how I respond to whatever comes to pass. Yet the nagging question remains: how do I live fully and to my greatest potential in the midst of a culture that believes that productivity equals worth?

Maybe I stay true to what I know is right despite the expectations and quantifications and market standards and hope that by doing so I can hold the energy that is needed to invite the change that is so needed in the world. Maybe I focus on the space that is in-between where I am and where I want to go, and maybe then I will notice that it's that in-between space that allows new things to come into being. Maybe from that space I can learn to recognize my gifts, and I can offer those gifts out into my community, my workplace, and my family. Maybe it is from my gifts—those gifts that are unique to my own being— that I can affect the "powers that be" in the deepest way and contribute to global healing. I might even say that giving up the notion that productivity equals worth is one of the essential puzzle pieces that could help fit peace into this world.

Zadie Smith says, "Tell the truth through whichever veil comes to hand—but tell it." Productivity doesn't equal worth. Can't get much more true than that.

As evident by that glimpse into my final corporate years, losing my job was a blessing and a curse, as the saying goes. As the company where I was employed grew, I had been getting increasingly burnt out and unhappy, to the point of crying when people were rude on the phone, and I even almost punched a wall on an especially bad day. I'm not a 'punch the wall' sort of person, as anyone in my inner circles can attest. People can be mean (to others and themselves) when feeling forced into a corner, and it's hard on the psyche to feel like you are being measured and evaluated constantly. I was glad to be stepping away from that part. I didn't want to be the version of myself that punched things out of frustration.

Instead, I wanted to look forward to my work days, to communicate in ways that resonated with people, and connect in ways that felt good to everyone involved in the exchange. I didn't want to follow strict protocols and mark the hours of the day by a back to back appointment schedule. I didn't want to pretend that business needs were priority when so many other things in the world dearly needed attention and energy. I was tired of trying to sell myself and prove my worth as an employee.

But the truth is that leaving somewhere (even if you need to for your sanity) on someone else's timetable makes life harder. Not having a corporate paycheck is less comfortable. This is probably obvious, but it makes me realize that I often took for granted the easy access to benefits that came as part of the package. I have a much greater understanding now about how important it is to have good, affordable healthcare available for all, no matter what your employment situation. Just because you work for a small company or a start-up that can't afford to provide affordable and adequate healthcare benefits doesn't mean you should have to spend half of your paycheck or monthly income to provide insurance for your family. Managing insurance shouldn't be so hard, and this from someone who doesn't have any serious health problems. I can only imagine the stress of having to choose between your diabetes medication and food.

One day as I was trying to sort through our health insurance mess, I had an encounter with a hummingbird. Dealing with the insurance stuff was making me anxious, even though we were all healthy and well. It was just the perceived "what ifs" that were causing fear and stress. Too much of our society is built on this energy of being afraid of what might happen, and we put so much of our life's work into safe-guarding ourselves "just in case." So health insurance eligibility issues were making me feel uncomfortable and scared, and they required multiple phone calls to sort out. But then I saw a hummingbird in the distance as I was drinking my coffee on the deck during a break from doing more research on our options. It was flying around just down the hillside, flitting from flower to flower, drinking nectar. The air was completely still, and as the tiny bird approached the house, I could hear its wings beating like a little motor. I stood still and waited for him to pass, but he didn't. He buzzed right up to the deck and hovered two inches from my nose as we looked each other in the eye for a few seconds. And in that moment, health insurance and the made-up threat that it represented faded into the still morning air, and I remembered that life on earth is so much more than fear of the "what ifs" and all of our human-made dramas.

It's worth saying that I have this perspective and the capacity to notice a hummingbird because of my privilege as a middle class white person in this country, who has had the good fortune of being born to loving parents who are still happily married and thriving. There's certainly nothing wrong with focusing on the things are beautiful and good, even in the midst of stressful situations. But that's the definition of privilege: to opt out of thinking or talking about something for awhile because you can.

Hummingbirds, nature, and practicing gratitude are important. So are basic human rights, peace, and changing our collective cultural narrative. I work hard to support myself and my family, and things are much more stressful when there is less money to go around and fewer affordable insurance options due to a job layoff. But I benefit daily from systemic racism and our country's broken history. You can't pull yourself up by your bootstraps and change how some people respond to you based on the color of your skin—privilege is not about how hard someone works. It's significantly harder to take time to listen to the flap of tiny wings while looking into the eyes of a hummingbird if you are born into a story that doesn't include the safety net that comes with privilege.

That morning I was reminded that even though I could be described as a person who had "lost their job" or one of our country's "unemployed," I have a safety net simply because of the life situation I was born into. I have the privilege of writing about whatever I want to write about from the comfort and safety of my home in an area with low crime and ample resources. Food on the table, safe streets to walk, healthy family members....these things are my reality, layoff or not. The shift in job status invited fear that those things would be harder to come by, perhaps, but they still remained.

If I've learned anything from all of this upheaval and uncertainty and sifting through what matters to me, I have learned that I don't want to find all of my life's meaning in my work. I want to do work that matters, to be sure, and I want to impact people in a positive way while contributing to the healing of the world. But I don't want to sacrifice my sanity to find a job that will do all of those things. Meaning has to come from somewhere deeper than what I do for a job.

Even several weeks after I got the news that my position was being eliminated, it still felt a little raw. It was unnerving, and I felt everything from bitter to empty to apathetic in the weeks leading up to my last day punching the clock. I felt like the rug had been pulled out from under me, leaving me strung out on a cold cement floor looking at the ceiling wondering what had happened. In my work over the last ten years I had been fortunate to feel effective, like I knew what I was doing, like my work mattered, and like I had what I needed to operate in the lifestyle that I'd chosen. But that day as I lay there looking at the ceiling, the threads that held my days together felt tenuous, kind of like it had all been a mirage. It felt my life had suddenly lost some of its meaning. It felt like the life I was living was about to slip through my fingers like sand.

In the United States, and I'd guess many other westernized nations, work has a tendency to be a defining feature of how we identify ourselves and how we measure our worth and value in the world. What we do 'for a living' tends to be a major influence in how we assign purpose to our lives. Being successful at work, for better or worse, matters in modern life. I learned the hard way that when work as we know it goes away, it's disorienting, even for those of us who think we know how to look deeper than a job to find life's purpose.

As I moved through those first weeks of being laid off, I was partially relieved to be moving into something different after all of those years struggling with burnout, but I was also terrified that I would discover that I wasn't equipped to do anything else. I was afraid I'd find that the jig was up and I'd been called out as a fraud; a failed experiment; not successful. I was afraid I'd discover that all these years I'd been trying to find my life's meaning in a job—but that it was just smoke and mirrors and perhaps my life didn't have any purpose after all.

In the weeks when I was a free agent, looking for new work, I felt adrift. My physical body got sick, probably due to all the anxiety that I was holding. The responsibility, the shame, the unworthiness, the feelings of being unwanted. All of these things can surely compound to make a person ill. Despite all of the free time I had, I felt like I wasn't pulling my weight, not doing enough. It sounds cliche to even write that, but there it is. It is harder to do things and feel productive (even though I know intellectually that productivity doesn't equate worth—knowing and accepting are sometimes different chapters) when no one is asking you to do something specific, giving you feedback, or paying you.

Yet there was so much good: new things to write about, a loving family, a place to live, a community, food on the table, clothes on my back, a fire in the woodstove. I learned that gratitude feels different when you've lost something that used to feel foundational. It was always easy before, something that I didn't really need to dig for. It's still easy to find things for which to give thanks, but it's harder to let the feeling of gratitude sink into my bones—harder to get to that place of deep knowing that my foundation is unshakable. Because, of course, I discovered that my foundation, or what I thought was my foundation anyway, is indeed shakable. I often still wonder, "How do I truly give thanks for the shaking?" Maybe acknowledging that I felt it being shaken was enough. Maybe it has forced me to use all my tools and ways of thinking that I'd been talking to coaching clients about over the years—the years when it was easy to take things for granted. An opportunity to practice what I preach. Maybe this was all just another layer of depth that somehow was adding meaning to my life.

As it happens, when I dig into what actually matters to me, I find meaning in listening to people, in helping others figure out how to take care of themselves, in spending time in the kitchen, in moving my body outside through the natural beauty that is present in the wilds of the world. I find meaning in the act of putting words together to make sense of an idea and in sitting with someone during a challenging time to simply bear witness. I find meaning in the sunrise, in the feel of the wind on my face as a storm moves in, and in the laughter of my child.

Many of these meaning makers had been present in my job, to be sure. As a health coach, most of my days were spent supporting people, listening, and being present. There has been plenty of meaning and

purpose in my work over the years, alongside the less desirable parts that tend to come with any job. But when the job was taken away, I found that the meaning was still there: when I planted a seed in the garden as the ground warmed in the spring or when I listened to the wind whistle across the frozen lake in the depths of winter. I found meaning every time I cooked a healthy meal for my family and when I shared the harvest with someone who needed it.

Anna Quindlen said it well when she advised, "Don't ever confuse the two, your life and your work. That's what I have to say. The second is only a part of the first." That job I held for ten years had been simply a slice of everything else that makes up my life. Even though there were feelings of anxiety, disappointment, and bitterness as my tenure came to an end, there were also feelings of curiosity, relief, and the sweet taste of what might be next right there with them.

I'm starting to think that a bit of shaking is what life needs to help meaning stand out, when all is said and done.

Writer Courtney E. Martin makes the helpful argument that our society is moving away from what was once considered "the good life." For years, people said things like "Well, I want my kids to be better off than I was," and often that meant hoping those kids got a steadier, better paying job, or a

bigger house in a nicer neighborhood, or into a more lucrative financial situation. I'm inclined to think that there's a cost to putting all of life's meaning under the old definition of "better off."

According to Martin's take on things, being "better off" doesn't always mean staying in one secure job forever and climbing the proverbial ladder to perceived success and material prosperity. I think "the new better off" means finding little bits of meaning in every portion of our lives and living from the feeling that comes from doing so. I am better off when I can spend my day feeling how I want to feel, not chasing a version of "better off" that is simply not better for what my soul wants. Better off for me is living each day in a way that fills me up, so I feel full of wonder and appreciation of beauty and light. I want to feel accomplished in the sense that what I do with my days matters and does something that contributes to the healing of the world. I want to make a positive impact on those with whom I interact, and that impact surely doesn't have to be the result of something that I get paid to do. But this is hard to balance in a world where money still holds the trump card more often than we want to admit. Privileged or not, bills don't just fade away with intention and positive thinking. (Or at least I'm not yet that spiritually evolved.) Striking the right balance takes persistence, support from a community, and perhaps a bit of luck.

No one's claiming that figuring out how to plug into life's meaning around, for lack of, or in spite of a job is easy. Identifying what "the new better off" looks like in a period of uncertainty is no picnic. Those last four weeks after getting the news that I was being laid off from what I thought was a very secure job after ten years of employment were some of the most challenging in my adult experience. When I had two weeks left to go before my position was officially "eliminated", it was really hard to keep showing up at work knowing every call I made was the last one, and that soon when someone asked me what I do for work, I wouldn't be sure what to say. But I felt better when I remembered Annie Dillard's words, "We can live any way we want. People take vows of poverty, chastity, and obedience—even of silence—by choice. The thing is to stalk your calling in a certain skilled and supple way, to locate the most tender and live spot and plug into that pulse. This is yielding, not fighting."

I'm learning that any work I do needs to be like that. It needs to be an avenue into stalking meaning in a way that locates that tender spot and then holds on tight to the pulse. The trick is to do my best to yield, not fight, when it comes to letting life's purpose in.

*

What do I want to yield to? What should I stalk in a way that adds value to my life, not just financial security? To what do I want to be devoted? Certainly not jobs that I don't like, the lure of social media, incessant negativity, or systems that take life away more than they give it. I want to be devoted to the sun, the moon, the rain, the stars. I want to be devoted to community, to the people I love, and to the gardens that feel so right, even when they present a challenge and I can't make things grow. I want to be devoted to beauty, to clean air, to good food, to joy. To the things that feel expansive and to the things that feel too small to be worth noticing. I want to be able to put my attention where it matters, not into a job that makes my soul tired and has me driving three hours a day to sit in a cubicle to follow someone else's protocol. My attention wants to be on telling stories, on empathizing with other beings, and on connecting with the parts of myself that are deeply woven into the natural world. I'm not interested in living in a way that makes me feel like a shell of myself, or pushing what I value aside just to make ends meet. David Whyte wrote, "You must learn one thing. The world was made to be free in. Give up all other worlds except the one to which you belong."

What world do I belong in? How do I get out of the worlds in which I do not belong? What beauty can be found in the challenge of uncertainty and doubt? What am I being called toward as I step away from what was?

*

This is what I want: A open, wide desk. Few items on the surface. A notebook, colored pencils, a small laptop computer. A cup of tea. A view to the left that lets me see the outdoors. Space to think and let thoughts flow into something else. Quiet. Peace. Room for all types of emotion and feeling. A safe place to let what wants to speak, speak. Bright sunshine during the day and soft lamplight by night. A space that feels right.

*

Something else I learned, or at least something else that was reinforced when I thought it might go away, is that I like working from home. I was very worried that to keep paying the bills I'd have to find a job in an office park somewhere in the city, and I even interviewed for one position that included a 60-mile one-way commute. I am deeply grateful that I didn't get that job, and that I found a work from home position (even if it was more hours that I wanted to devote to just one job) that allowed me to continue to spend my days at home in the woods.

A new job. Good for the bank account, and hopefully good for the soul as well. Coaching again, but no phone time and no strict schedule. But 40 hours a week. I don't want to spend 40 hours a week at a job. Grateful. But how to find the right balance? Will I just burn out again? I really want to like this new job. I want it to be a good fit for me and enough to sustain our family's needs. I want to not get lost in the demands of a 40 hour week—after ten years of 32 hours a week, 40 feels like too much. Life feels hard. And then it feels easy. And then hard. And then somewhere in the middle. It is constantly evolving and changing course, even when it feels like nothing will ever change.

Week four of the new job. I like it.

I want that to be ok.

I'm afraid I'm taking the easy way out and that I should keep looking. Or start my own business, work for myself. Or move to an off grid yurt in the northwoods. Or find buried treasure in the backyard.

*

I watched a robin explore one of our crabapple trees one February afternoon a few weeks after my severance pay ran out. The robin hopped from bare branch to bare branch, stopping now and then to poke at old, dried-up crabapples with his beak. At one point he seemed to look right at me, kind of like that hummingbird had, as if he were making sure I noticed his presence. (There's something about birds.) I wasn't sure how to respond.

Robins usually don't come back to this area of Minnesota until at least the end of March, though last few years we've seen them as early as February, and that year on the same day I saw the robin, the 'spring melt' stream ran—both things unseasonably early. The snow was almost gone after a few days of 40 degrees, and that day was it was 50. The next day it was projected to be 55, and Sunday that week, 57. Winter as I remember it just wasn't happening, and this early warmth didn't feel normal.

I started the new job that week, too (the universe had my back with that one)—it was a lot of meetings and figuring out passwords and learning new technology and exploring websites. The job itself was familiar—the basic practice of coaching people into a healthier way of being doesn't change even when the organization you work for does. When boiled down, coaching is an opportunity to help people see all the options they have in their own lives, and it's an opportunity to help them cultivate the behaviors that will result in living true to what they value. The structure at the new place was different than the corporate environment that defined my days for almost a decade. There was more room for flexibility, creativity, and making use of the writing skills I have developed over the years. If I'm being honest, I'd ideally spend the bulk of my days writing books, planning the garden, or hiking with my daughter. But since there are still bills to pay and my skill set aligns with using writing to communicate with clients, this job turned out to be one of the better options that crossed my path. But it was new. It didn't feel normal. A fear of burning out again still lingered.

The climate isn't what it used to be—this isn't a new phenomenon, of course. The climate has always shifted. But now it's shifting faster than anyone thought it would, and it's shifting for different reasons than it has in the past. Most of what happens with the temperature outdoors (to grossly oversimplify) is outside of our control, even though human activity has played a large role in getting us where we are. But we are where we are, and it can be hard to know how to respond. We have to figure out how to deal with the reality we are in.

As I moved into the first weeks of making a new coaching job a part of my life, I wasn't sure how to respond. Part of me was relieved to have found another telecommuting opportunity. Part of me was lamenting the fact that I had a schedule to adhere to again, even if it was fairly flexible. And part of me was ready to simply take things one day at a time and figure out how to deal with the reality that I was in.

And as February progressed and another winter seemed to fade before it really even began, I wasn't sure how to respond. Part of me was relieved to have sun warming my face as I stood on the south facing hills in the afternoon. Part of me was lamenting the fact that skiing was probably over for the year, and another warm winter meant that climate change was starting to have a real impact on my day to day life. And part of me was ready to simply take things one day at a time and figure out how to deal with the reality that I was in.

*

Later that spring, I woke up to the April snowfall that still comes almost every year—even these last few, when it seems winter just isn't what it used to be. I walked down to the dock as the sun got higher, mostly covered by clouds, and I marveled at the reflection that is possible when the water is glassy and the lake is still weed-free. The birds were singing, and the snow was starting to drip off the branches. I was reminded, once again, why it makes me happy to live in this place where woods meet water, in a little red house that sits imperfectly perched between two ravines. There is life all around, and there is beauty to be found even in a spring snowfall at a time when I'm ready to plant the garden instead.

The days and weeks seemed to fly by as we sat in this place of impermanence and uncertainty. My new job was a good fit, as jobs go, but it didn't pay well. There was still lingering doubt that we could afford to stay in our house and keep up with all the repairs that were needed. My spouse was considering a job with a commute that would take him into the city every day of the week, after years of staying home to care for our young daughter, and we were struggling with the ramifications of the options available, none of which seemed good. Potential for even more drastic change swirled around us, yet we somehow moved through the days one at a time.

It felt like we were waiting for something to shift, or to feel more stable. But there is always something to wait for, and there is always more to come. There is never a perfect moment or opportunity or answer. There is only what happens and how we respond with the choice that needs to come next.

Even months after I got that new job, we remained in that strange time of uncertainty and simply not knowing what the next season would bring. Finances remained more stressful than they ever had been as we continued to discern whether or not my new employment situation was enough to sustain our homestead that was purchased on a budget that had been underwritten by a corporation. It felt like hard work. It's possible to do hard things, but this felt really hard. It felt like destruction was always just right around the next corner.

That summer, I was sitting outside on the back deck, surrounded by towering basswood trees that had just fully come into their summer leafy glory. Birds were chirping, and I could hear frogs croaking in the shallows of the lake, and squirrels chattering at each other as they raced from tree to tree. Filtered sunlight was streaming down, there was a gentle breeze keeping the bugs away, the delicate purple flowers of the hillside Sweet William were in full bloom, and all of this created a little oasis of beauty and tranquility. I could also hear the growl of heavy machinery as crews prepared to pave another section of our road, and every so often there'd be a loud crash as a tree came down, followed by the buzzing of a chainsaw and the beeping of a large loader backing up. I heard a diesel truck roar by and the dust from the road rose like a massive cloud as it raced by the house. Beauty and destruction are strange bedfellows, yet they coexist next to each other all the time.

Then one unseasonably cold and rainy day in August meant that it was time to pause. It was too wet to work in the garden, the road crews had to take a break due to incessant downpours, and time in the kitchen didn't feel like work when I trying to find ways to stay warm and nourished. As the earth drank in refreshment from the rain, I looked for ways to do the same by taking this cue from nature. There is always more to do, more to worry about, more to lament, more to plan. But I, just like we all do, need to take time to replenish, too, or I run the risk of burning out on life just like I did at corporate coaching.

As the years progress, with them have come plenty of chances to be where I am and to lean into reality. I once heard former grief counselor Stephen Jenkinson say, "I just started being where I was." I often wonder why that is so difficult, and if it has always been hard for humans. I wonder if it has only become hard with the rise of technology and the faster pace of life that comes with it. Maybe it wasn't so challenging to be fully present years ago without so much beckoning at the same time. But, then again, maybe not. Maybe humans have always struggled with this and we just tell ourselves that technology is at fault instead of looking at ourselves.

Jenkinson also said, "I just stopped being where I wasn't." That's something to aspire to. I wonder what it would really take to be present. No computer? No iPhone? No planner? No job? Would it take more "no"? Or perhaps more "yes"—yes to focus, yes to one thing at a time, yes to noticing the details of the hours, yes to slowing down, yes to doing and wanting less. Yes to letting the need for excess validation and approval go. Yes to doing and accepting hard things and learning from the scars that are left behind.

One evening mid-summer that first year after the job loss, I went out to pick the last of the day's ripe blueberries, and as I was lingering in the garden enjoying the cool dusky air, I noticed the sunflowers.

In the last week, four of them had grown almost as tall as me and were starting to show signs of blossoming. Their heads were still tight in a bud, but I could tell they were eagerly waiting the day when they could show their petals to the sun. Somehow there was medicine in those buds—in what they were in the moment, and in what they might become someday in the future.

It's easy to forget what the earth can offer when it comes to navigating challenging situations: from physical cures in the form of a tincture to emotional respite that comes from noticing the beauty in a sunflower for longer than a passing second. Sometimes I feel silly when I get caught up in something like a sunflower—after all, there are important things to do, like answering emails or looking for a better job or financial planning or organizing the hall closet. I think it's because I don't like to feel exposed. Reveling in the beauty of a sunflower reveals something about me that can feel dangerous to show to the world. After all, it exposes my values and what truly matters to me, and that, though essential for a full life, is scary.

Sharman Apt Russell writes, in a book titled Anatomy of a Rose, about her feelings of embarrassment when spending time naked in some hot springs, and she's certainly not alone in that. I would have a hard time, too, as she did, standing naked outside and drinking in the healing properties of nature, instead of being preoccupied with how my body looked or felt in its exposed state. It's more comfortable to stay covered up, even when there's no one else around. It's easier to skim the surface than to go deep enough to let the healing of something like a flower do its work in us.

It hasn't been easy to navigate this time of upheaval, and in fact, it's often felt like standing naked outside on a sunny day. Losing something central to modern life—like a job—has made me feel exposed and vulnerable. But it's also made me realize that it's possible to heal from such an event and that wildness and nature and learning to lean into the ashes of what has burned away have a place in the journey.

As Russel writes, "We may need to be cured by flowers. We may need to strip naked and let the petals fall on our shoulders, down our bellies, against our thighs. We may need to walk naked through beauty. [...] We may need to feel beauty on our skin. We may need to walk the pollen path, among the flowers that are everywhere."

No life situation is permanent. Losing a job that felt really secure was unsettling, and it continually reminds me that there are no guarantees in life. Things can change in a blink of an eye, and we can't ever know what might be coming next. But we can learn to pay attention to what serves us and prioritize those things, and we can use each hardship to build the resilience we need for whatever challenges lie ahead. And the meaning that we find outside of our day jobs? That's what sticks around. That has staying power, even while the circumstances of life change.

What does come next? I can't know. But there is always a choice in how the story unfolds, even if it is only found in how I respond to something completely outside of my control.

There is beauty and there is destruction, and they are existing side by side. This is not new—it's been happening since the dawn of time. It will keep happening for the rest of my human lifetime. So my plan is to take the beauty that I find wherever I am, whatever my employment status, whatever life decides to dish out next, and use it to fuel myself with active hope. To focus on what I can control, notice the beauty of the earth, and refuse to let someone speak for me if I don't agree with what they are saying. To use my privilege in ways that are life-giving. To let the contrasts that tend to define life illuminate the options that are there when I am ready to uncover them. To build my capacity to lead in the quiet ways that suit best. To come to my senses, and let my life be strengthened by the persistent beauty of the world.

So, that's that. Lessons from a layoff, you might call it. Every year those strong autumn winds will blow, and I will see the yellow and orange leaves fall to the ground. The beauty of the season will always fade, but I'm reminded that beauty doesn't always look how I think it should. I'm starting to think beauty is best uncovered in the rubble of destruction. Perhaps that's what comes next.

HEIDI BARR (SHE/HER) is a writer and wellness coach whose work is founded on a commitment to cultivating ways of being that are life-giving and sustainable for people, communities, and the planet. She is the author of several books of creative nonfiction, including *Collisions of Earth and Sky and Woodland Manitou,* and co author of *12 Tiny Things.* She's also authored three poetry collections, one cookbook, and is editor of "The Mindful Kitchen," a wellness column in *Wayfarer Magazine.* One of the inaugural Poets of Place for the lower St. Croix Valley, her poetry has been featured in numerous publications, including the *St. Paul Almanac and South Dakota in Poems.* She lives with her family in rural Minnesota, where they tend a large vegetable garden, explore nature, and do their best to live simply.

POINT YOURSELF IN THE DIRECTION OF THE SUNSET

INTERVIEW WITH KASHAWN TAYLOR
BY HEIDI BARR

The forces in our lives are constantly colliding—sometimes in ways that work out well and sometimes in ways that don't. This interview series is an exploration of what it can look like to work with the collisions, rather than against them. By digging into how humans and nature interact- from our relationships with other humans, to those with our non-human neighbors, to our relationship with ourselves to our relationship with the landbase-we can uncover how to best step fully into our role in the story of the world.

Kashawn is a formerly incarcerated writer based in Connecticut. His work has been or will be published by such journals and magazines as *The Blotter, Indiana Review, Querencia Press, Poetry Magazine, Miracle Monocle, The Offing,* and more. His debut collection of poetry, *subhuman.,* will be published in March 2025 by Wayfarer Books.

HEIDI: Kashawn, thanks for being here with us today. To start, I always ask the same question: What are two forces that are colliding in your life right now (or that have in the not too distant past)?

KASHAWN: What a great question, and for me, a simple one. Right now, I am straddling the fence between incarceration and full freedom. I am currently on what is known as community release after a twenty-one month stint in prison for a car accident where someone lost their life. It was honestly a life-changing experience. Now, living under supervision, I am trying to get back into being a real person again, writing my experience, working, and going back to school for an MFA after my MA.

HEIDI: It sounds like you're living in what's sometimes called that "space between stories"— both a challenging and illuminating time. How are you navigating the conditions this collision is creating? How does the dissonance created impact your choices?

KASHAWN: I think with so much looming over my shoulder—my past, possible re-incarceration, and the stigma that comes along with having been to prison—I have been navigating the conditions well. I'm much more focused than I ever was. I'll be thirty-two in about a month; I graduated from my undergrad in 2013 and did nothing with writing until I went to prison. Since getting out, I have been more tenacious in honing my craft which includes fiction, poetry, and nonfiction. I have been able to get more writing done and submitted without the distractions. My life right now is very structured, and I kind of love it. When I am not working, I use my free time to write, do school work, and work out. Overall, I make better choices having known where bad decisions can lead me, and with those better choices comes the space to make art.

HEIDI: It does sound like you're navigating just fine—you're using your past experience to fuel your current reality. I love this: "..with those better choices comes the space to make art." You're setting yourself up for creativity with all that focus—what a gift to yourself and your readers.

What has this collision taught you about yourself? The world?

KASHAWN: That I can do things when I set my mind to them. When I allow doubt and insecurity to creep in, I become immobile. I get anxious and do nothing. Then, I feel bad about doing nothing. It's a vicious cycle, really. Things can get done—on small and large scales—if we work towards them, one step at a time. Even if they are baby steps. I am an optimist at heart. I believe in the good in people, in the world. When I think about where I came from, the lows that I have faced, the pain that I have caused, and where I am now, the difference is night and day. This world is sad, but it's also really good and beautiful, and sometimes people just need to be pointed in the direction of the sunset instead of standing with their back to the beauty.

This world is sad, but it's also really good and beautiful, and sometimes people just need to be pointed in the direction of the sunset instead of standing with their back to the beauty.

HEIDI: I love that last sentence about pointing ourselves in the direction of beauty so much. And as a fierce advocate of the power of tiny, intentional acts, I appreciate you sharing that those small steps is how change is made.

Now, I'd love to hear about a collision you explore in your latest project.

KASHAWN: A collision I explore in subhuman. is the relationship between myself and those on the outside. I write a lot about how the world moves on, how people stop answering the phone, and how relationships change when a person is incarcerated. There are lots of feelings of loneliness though I was surrounded by lots of people, many of whom I still keep in contact with today. Relationships are a big theme in the book: relationships with those on the outside, with other inmates, and with myself. Feeling resigned versus making the best of my experience, hating myself versus trying to better myself. Now that I think of it, there are so many collisions in the book.

HEIDI: I look forward to reading about them very much when the collection comes out next spring. From what you've shared, I think it's a book that's going to speak to so many folks—from loneliness to trying to navigate relationships to feeling left behind. There is so much important stuff that you're unpacking.

HEIDI: As we wrap up today, what else would you like to share about your current projects?

KASHAWN: I have so many fun things in the pipeline. "The Court Trip" is an essay that will be out November 14th, published by The Offing. In December, Miracle Monocle will be publishing a short story called "Dead Air." *Emergent Literary, Poetry Magazine,* and *Words Beyond Bars* have some selections from *subhuman.* that will be published in the coming months. Some recent publications include: *BULL Lit Mag, The Shore Poetry,* and *Union Spring Literary Review.* And of course, *subhuman.* will be out in March 2025 which is something I am so proud of.

SAD FRUIT

By Kashawn Taylor

Apples here taste so bitter,

copper, like chewing a battery

or a secret lover's bottom lip;

angry apples, determined to,

at the same time,

nourish and punish.

I imagine the destitute orchard

from which they come,

the desperate trees on which they grow.

How the soil might taste

if I consumed a moist, grainy handful,

broke my teeth on stones

and the bones of small animals

cursed to rest in the eldritch pasture.

Would my roots wither,

become petrified tendrils, arms

fingering for loamy sustenance?

Would my trunk grow strong,

a redoubtable oaken bulwark,

or would it fail, and fall

like the Wall in its sole task?

Could my leaves withstand the gale,

the fusillade of rain, the sunshine-

joy and two AM-doom of summer?

My bark yearns

to be hugged before nuclear

autumn, before small animals shelter

and the birds ride prevailing winds south.

If there was a little love,

the raven smoke from these fires

which choke and erase

might give birth to new beginnings,

a phoenix-resurrection for

the sad fruit I give to this sad world.

It is true:

our roots dictate our growth,

but even those can be excavated,

then replanted.

It is our seeds which float

the lightest breeze, that roam

farther than our dying, browning

leaves and leave flavors

—bitter or sweet?—

on the puckered lips of lives

we never come close to kissing.

//

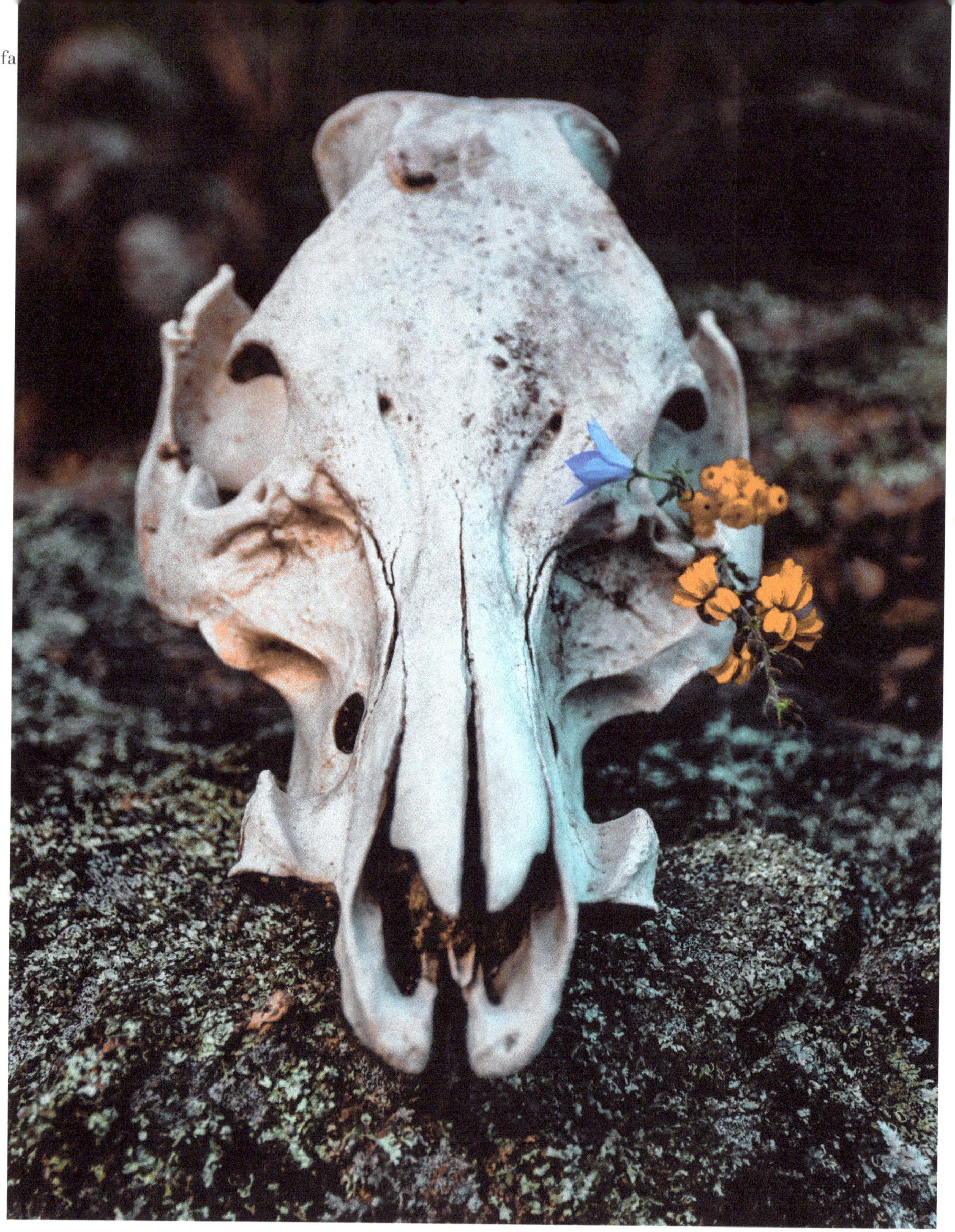

POETRY

Connor Wolfe
FEATURED

Walker Abel

Gary Whited

Will Falk

Robert Broder

Jackie Moloney

Rick Benjamin

Mubanga Kalimamukwento

Jose Oseguera

Rebecca Dietrich

C.W. Emerson

Michael Garrigan

Janna Knittel

Rebecca Brenner

Gwendolyn Morgan

70

PHOTO BY JORDON CONNER

THE SUBTERRANEANS

BY CONNOR WOLFE

» Cerro Pedernal, NM.
  Night of the Election 2024.

We walk where roots twist,
where rivers hum ancient songs,
where light bends, refusing
the clean symmetry of the surface.

Up there, they press lives into molds,
worship at the altar of sameness—
words sterilized, dreams shelved.

But down here, the air is raw,
electric with unscripted truths.
Hearts beat to the rhythm of refusal,
whispers echo like thunder.
Call us lost, call us strange—
we've touched the earth's marrow
and will not crawl back.

We rise from the cracks,
the places they paved over.
Their shiny cities hum compliance,
trading freedom for comfort,
nights lit by screens
selling back their emptiness.

Down here, we are roots,
snaking beneath their towers,
breaking through stone.
Our voices rise—a swelling tide,
not silenced by laws, borders,
walls of glass and steel.

You don't know how far down you've gone
until their world burns,
a kingdom of fear, paper-thin.
Let it burn.

We are the underground fire,
the poets, the dreamers,
the queers, the marginalized,
the ones who refuse
to surrender the night.

FIND ME IN THE LOBBY
BY CONNOR WOLFE

You never danced—
said you would, but you slipped
'round the corner, at the Algonquin,
that old haunt, that no-questions bar,
and the all-night diner glowing greasy in the dark,
buzzing neon and coffee steam, a little lonely,
tucked by Bryant Park where the city breathes out,
and the streets run on fumes and echoes

It was just me there—
me and the girl from the North Country—
waiting on something, leaning on the night,
building a window with a thrifted frame

waiting on a song that never came,
waiting on a tune that only the city knew,
like a lost word, like a whisper, like a beat
you can't hold onto, like a night
that fades before you get the ending.

GENUS SAYORNIS
BY CONNOR WOLFE

I brought blackberries
to feed you—
one
by
one.

After you left,
they tangled into thickets,
wild on the 'stead,
spoiled
in the summer sun—
one
by
one.

Cutting them back,
bloodied by brambles,
the birds cried your name.

CONNOR WOLFE (THEY/THEM) is the Founder of Wayfarer Books & Wayfarer Magazine. Wolfe's innovative approach to independent publishing led to two terms on the Board of Directors for the Independent Book Publishers Association, a TEDx talk at Yale University, and studies at Harvard University through grant programs.

After delivering a TEDx talk in 2018 about their experiences with successive trauma, Wolfe was invited to participate in broader mental health discussions at state and national levels. They hold a degree in Abnormal Psychology from Harvard University, with a focus on the intersection of mental illness and creativity. Driven by their passion for art, Wolfe pursued a minor in Photojournalism at Harvard, studying under Samantha Appleton, former Official White House Photographer for President Obama and the First Family.

In early 2024, Wolfe worked as volunteer staff in the Collections Department of the Museum of Anthropology at Ghost Ranch, assisting a team preparing sacred objects for repatriation under the newly updated Native American Graves Protection and Repatriation Act. They are currently wintering along the Rio Puerco on Cerro Pedernal.

Follow their Substack for the latest: thewildwolfe.substack.com

ROOTWORK OF THE BONE
BY CONNOR WOLFE

I am the knife
And the wound,
And the salt,

The nerve that flinches,
The cry that echoes,
    threaded through the silence.

I am the shadow carved by a winter sun,
A name spoken with a ghost's tongue
    and forgotten.

I am the bloom of the yucca,
Wounded—
    and still reaching for the sky.

I am the hunger of wolves beneath a frozen moon,
The smoke that curls from burned bridges,
The quiet, feral thing that lives in the ruins.

I am the question that silence asks,
The answer hidden in the rootwork of the bone
A call flung toward the faceless sky,

I am the breaking,
And the breaking open.

TRANS-FORMATION
BY CONNOR WOLFE

It is the queer's alchemy—
to turn the shame
into swagger.

CONFESSIONS FROM
A FORMER CONTORTIONIST
BY CONNOR WOLFE

Not until you're sprawled—
in the open, limbs unbound,
upended,
    stretching wide—
do you feel it, know it:
how that box kept shrinking,
how you'd coiled yourself tight,
twisted bone and breath
to fit their narrow frame.

THE OLD GODS
BY CONNOR WOLFE

Just when I thought,
God is dead—again.
They grew wings
And became a hawk.

THE ONE ABOUT THE GIRL AND THE CLOSET

BY TYLER HURULA

a girl walks into her mother's closet & says she's bisexual & the mother hands her a shirt to fold & says *you won't feel that way in ten years* & the girl walks into her boyfriend's arms & says she likes girls & the boy laughs & hands her his cock & the girl starts dating a woman & when her father asks if she's found a boy at college she gives him the woman's name & he repeats it three times, *Britta Britta Britta* & looks around like she'll parade out of a mirror, Birkenstocks first, preaching the good word of the Indigo Girls, before demanding she not tell her sisters & the girl comes out as polyamorous & her mother fumes an angry message to the girl's now wife—something about cheating & the girl tells her best friend she's dating two people & they're all happy & enamored & everyone who has only ever committed to one person at a time collectively chimes in & says *I could never do that while* 51% of them file for divorce & the best friend asks about jealousy while loving both her daughters & then ghosts the girl & the girl tells her queer friend she's dating someone whose pronouns are they & them & the queer friend laughs & *says thank God, I was beginning to think you were straight* & a primitive boy on a dating app tells the girl he's fantasizing about her & his wife & the girl is fucking tired of coming out & explaining she's not here to perform & shrugs off her validation butch & snaps six promise rings from her fingers & bites her tongue clean through & braces herself for the punchline but there is none & she bludgeons her feet against the floor & she shrieks herself hollow & last anyone's heard she's still slamming her fists against an echoing closet door

I'VE ONLY BEEN TOLD I'M HARD TO READ BY PEOPLE I DON'T LIKE

BY TYLER HURULA

I once had a thirty-seven hour first date & maybe that's the lesbian

in me, but I like to say I'm a pansy petaled with questions

like what was the name of your first Subaru? or how would you describe

your attachment style? Being with me is like going to a year-long

music festival, but it's only one song on repeat. One lover built

an advent calendar for my birthday & said the only

other person who gets an advent calendar for their birthday

is Jesus & maybe one day I'll walk on wine—I mean water,

but I like to pretend I can tell the difference between an oaky

finish & a hint of vanilla in the former. My boss said I have a gift

for being direct & it is off-putting. I've tattooed Brutus on my face

for all the times it's betrayed me & I've only been told I'm hard

to read by people I don't like.

I am pomegranate punch hair. Profane. Petty. Punctual—

or at least I used to be. I wear my heart as anatomically correct

rosé-colored glasses & I am pretty poet pink with jeweled

teeth & I personified my too much in a poem to separate

myself from the reason people have left me. I threw out the manual

on subtlety & mistake clever for vulnerable, so I clever up my feelings

& write them out & revise them. Little logic heart. I am not tender

step, more like a thump & one time I fell down the stairs & landed

with my foot in my mouth & covered in bruises & laid there until I cried

out *I'm okay* for no one but me. I won't get out of here unscathed.

I only buy lipstick that isn't supposed to smudge or fade, but the truth

is I will leave a stain that cannot be mistaken for accidental.

TYLER HURULA (SHE/THEY) is the pinkest poet in Denver, Colorado. She strives to be the most queer and polyamorous person they can be. Author of *Love Me Louder* (Querencia Press). She has been nominated for Best of the Net and Pushcart Prizes. Her next collection, *Too Pretty for Plain Coffee*, is forthcoming from Wayfarer Books. Find her on Instagram @theprettypinkpoet.

HOW WE GOT HERE
BY WILL FALK

You were never meant
to carry the weight of the world,
but I bet you can carry more
than you currently are.
The gaze of that orphaned
Sumatran orangutan,
her tiny toes clinging
to the last tree the machines
didn't eat, suggests it doesn't
really matter if you can or can't.

You must.

Being the change
you wish to see in the world
never worked for those peoples
who never really needed to change
but who were still in the way
after pox painted their skin red
and the price of scalps
rose to five dollars
a bloody head.

Those wandering ghosts,
missing half their hair,
insist that change is
not to be until it is made.

You may have been taught
to value a kitten or a puppy
more than a calf or a piglet
but beetles have babies, too,
streams dream of one day

reaching the ocean
like their river mothers,
and soil is sick
of being treated like dirt.

You should not doubt
that a small group of thoughtful,
committed citizens
can change the world.
It's just that
the ones who have
have a lot more money
and a lot more weapons than you.

Termites, fueling their bodies
by feeding on wood,
until the whole house collapses
prove that the master's tools
can indeed dismantle
the master's house.
But anyone who has ever
actually picked up a chainsaw
knows that the only possession
the saw respects is the one
who pulls the trigger.

And, of course, violence never works
said no conqueror ever.
And that little orangutan,
those scalped ghosts, and
millions of beetle mothers
mourning their babies
demand to know:

if it wasn't for violence,
how did we get here?

WILL FALK (HE/HIM) is a biophilic activist, author, and attorney. The natural world speaks and poetry is how Will listens. His law practice is devoted to helping Native American communities protect their sacred sites and cultural resources. He is the author of *How Dams Fall* and *When I Set the Sweetgrass Down.* willfalk.org.

EVEN YAHWEH

BY WILL FALK

I try to flee the news from Gaza
on interstates west across Indiana,
Illinois, Iowa, and Nebraska.
The corn and cottonwoods
show me there is no
earthly refuge from the truth.

There were bison here, once.
But God's chosen ones
could not reap what they sowed
until the Oto, Cheyenne, and Arapahoe
were starved out of the way.

Now the only buffalo
you'll find on the great plains
are ones stuffed in pioneer museums.
Their original hunters – not the ones
who slaughtered the beasts
with repeating rifles from railcars,
took only the hides and
stacked the skulls five stories high –
are stuffed into dust bowls
that boomed sooner than
Oklahoma oil pipelines.

Even Yahweh, they say,
stole his fair share of land.
Ask Goliath and his Philistines.

So, I do. And all I find
is the ashes of bombed out buildings
sprinkled like powdered sugar
on deep fried lies, broken babies
scattered on piles of shattered bones,
and a cold, October wind that
blows through the bile of
my ever-boiling belly
to harden my words like lead
into bullets robbed from me
for David's new long range sling.

OLIVE

BY RICK BENJAMIN

Fruit fractal,
        seed & roots,
                oil pressed
into the past
        imperfect, 8
                million trees
a decade ago
        cultivated, occupied
                land, liberated
crop. Olive groves
        in evidence 4
                thousand years
before Jesus tried
        to heal the human
                once & for all.
The call to prayer
        can wake up a whole
                city, can call you to
wake up any time of day:
        it's harvest time, there's
                fruit to pick. The air heavy
& rich with oil. Until, at
        last there isn't any, no trees
                or people that haven't been
bulldozed or bombarded to death.
        The Palestinians, they are olive
                people, just as the Salish are salmon.
Every olive leaf
        is a skeleton; every
                human life carries a trace
of evidence, of kinship with
        the more-than-human world,
                & that tree will, again, bear fruit.

QUEERDOM

BY RICK BENJAMIN

latest dispatches from inner ear

Headlines today: most erotic moment
when sun hit face, left cheek still in a
state of ecstasy;

    : humans—only species
reducing erotic to something sexual
or gendered;

    : meanwhile breeze
entered ear, caressed & teased membrane
we call, drum, until percussive hum exited
that sonic cavern, cave, tunneling its way
back out into trees & dry fall leaves where
they continued to rustle;

    : when someone thinks
they should govern desire or identity
or insist on any of the binaries, both
human & more-than-human they
should be summarily deposed
by the whole sentient world
&, in the event of shyness
on part of humans, all
other species will
affirm this, one,
Constitutional;

    : tribunals along
lines of reconciliation
shall govern
the days & nights; making amends,
asking for forgiveness (no matter
the outcomes); crow caws (tercets
& quatrains mostly), & same inter-
vals between calls, are well worth
listening to (murders generally
knowing what they're on about);

    : mexican purple
sage round here attracts all of the
hummers, bees, hovering birds. A
whole bush can vibrate with all
of that sweetness.

    : that ear drum's
all scar tissue tbh; a thinner skin
was ruptured long ago & that low
drone you've been straining to
hear's the queerest thing you'll
ever hold.

RICK BENJAMIN (HIM/HE), former state poet laureate of Rhode Island, teaches at the University of California, Santa Barbara, offering courses in poetry, ecological literature, juvenile justice, and community engagement in the Comparative Literature and Environmental Studies departments. He has also taught at Brown University, RISD, Goddard College, and in diverse community settings with people aged six to ninety-six. The author of five poetry collections, his latest is The Mob Within The Heart (Wayfarer Books, 2021). He lives on unceded Chumash land in Goleta, California.

ANOTHER MOTHER DOES NOT COME WHEN YOURS DIES

BY MUBANGA KALIMAMUKWENTO

I learn how to pray on my mother's lap. We are at Bible study, as we are every Friday evening in the pastor's house, surrounded by people I see on Fridays and then again on Sundays during the main service. My mother always starts these evenings quiet, only Shani-ing and Bwino, shani-ing between handshakes with the other adults in a whisper. Then she pulls her concentration face–lips pursed– and nods at everything the pastor says even though he tells zigzagging stories about lips-shut lions, talking shrubs, and direct conversations with God.

The smell of eat-sum-more biscuits and milked tea wafts up from the glass coffee table in the middle of the sitting room. I'm sure everyone's stomach is grumbling, not just mine. But the routine is, no one moves to pick either biscuit or teacup until Amai Busa, the pastor's wife, offers the tray just before we leave when the tea is too cold and the biscuits have hardened around the edges.

The first time we came here, I raised my hand to ask a question. My mother chuckled, pulling it down, telling me afterwards That's not how things are done, even though I'd heard her tell the pupils she tutored that, questions were how we learnt.

I want to ask if the lion's mouth was shut with a zipper or a lock, why no one thought to pour water on that poor shrub, and what number is God's because I like memorizing phone numbers. But I remain quiet, remembering how my mother says, Once is for the instruction, the second will be a slap, and rub my cheek as if it is already stinging.

My mother has no questions and only breaks her reverie by mouthing her Amen. The pastor is talking about a marriage between repentance and forgiveness at this point, explaining that the children of that marriage are blessings like he and his wife enjoy now. He points to the chandelier with its knife-sharp prisms, at their daughter, Hosanna, who is reading a children's Bible next to her mother, and then at his car keys laid next to the biscuits and cooling tea. I watch his fat pointer finger float from blessing to blessing and conjure this God as a fairy, blessing and blessing and blessing.

Amen, goes my mother's mouth. Her breath, still pepperminty because she insists on us brushing our teeth before we leave the house, kisses me lightly on my head.

This sermon–like the ones before–ends with the same series of promises of restoration, that God will rebuild whatever area of our lives had been eaten by termites, the way he did for Joseph and for Hannah and for Jacob and Sarah.

Hallelujah! Preach it! Glory! and Amen! jump out from the adults' mouths like fireflies. This is where my mother's voice steps in, warm as freshly fried vitumbuwa, round as the hug she has me enveloped in. She joins in the incantations, the first of the adults to flee English and dip into a language of her own fabrication, but no one minds. They start down parallel paths of gibberish, which my mother told me is called speaking in tongues. I shut my eyes. The way their tongues crash into each other reminds me too much of the rainy season's first thunder, how, even though November petrichor warns of its coming, my heart never fails to jolt at the sound. I always run to hide under the blankets as if they can shield me from the rapid, incessant booming.

The vibrations of my mother's voice through her chest drum against my ears, climbing louder and louder until, just when I think whatever holds sounds in it will split at the seams, she stops with a tear-stained Amen. I can speak six languages: English–because my teacher whips anyone who doesn't speak it; Bemba–for my nanny, who has been with us since before my memory crystallized; French, which my mother teaches at the Girls Secondary School near the town fence; and enough Tonga, Nyanja, and Luvale for all the grown-ups who hear me to fawn and say Wow, such a clever girl. But what language does God speak, one of my six or one of these tongues? I wonder if mouthing along with my mother would count as my seventh, even though I can't entirely untangle the meaning from the sounds.

Whatever language God speaks, it is not one of these because my mother will come to this Bible study waiting for the restoration promise until I've outgrown her lap.

MUBANGA KALIMAMUKWENTO (SHE/HER) is a Zambian attorney, editor, and writer. She is the author of *The Mourning Bird* (Jacana), *unmarked graves* (Tusculum University Press), *Obligations to the Wounded* (University of Pittsburgh Press), *Another Mother Does Not Come When Yours Dies* (Wayfarer Books) and *Shipikisha* (forthcoming from Dzanc Books). She has an MFA in creative writing from Hamline University, is the founding editor of *Ubwali Literary Magazine*, a 2024 Miles Morland Scholar, and a PhD student and Interdisciplinary Center for the Study of Global Change (ICGC) scholar at the University of Minnesota Twin Cities.

HE SLEEPS BETWEEN HER BREASTS

BY JOSE OSEGUERA

As twilight shows how this sweet corrosion begins to be complete—
from "How We Made a New Art on Old Ground" by Eavan Boland

I watch with the utmost fear

as our son climbs the bars of his crib,

after the milk is gone, and stands up

for the baby cam only minutes after

my wife laid him in his crib

with a bottle and an Ave Maria.

We pick him up and place him in his walker,

he runs unhindered as if on the surface of the moon:

one small step for little man,

one giant leap for her weary mind.

He scuddles to the kitchen

to drum on the trash can— his treasure—

he lifts the lid, pulls on its liner, a big bang.

We run to see what happened:

dust and rubbish spread all over the floor,

my son, the axis of this chaos.

As he rolls around this big crunch

of egg shells and empty popcorn bags,

she walks to him— Mother Earth growing closer to her sun.

They give up the chase, the revolution—

they embrace destruction, each other—

colliding with the inevitable

he sleeps between her breasts.

This nebula of heat,

his body— a jewel no longer

traveling through light and dark and light again—

her body, renewed, as when they were one source,

a single glimmer in space.

JOSE OSEGUERA (HE/HIM) is the author of the poetry collection *The Milk of Your Blood* (Kelsay Books). His poems have appeared in *Chautauqua, Sonora Review, North Dakota Quarterly, Catamaran* and elsewhere. He was named one of the *Sixty Four Best Poets of 2019* by the Black Mountain Press. He was the recipient of the Nancy Dew Taylor Award in 2019 and placed 2nd in the 2020 Hal Prize Contest. His writing has been nominated for the Best of the Net award (2018, twice in 2019) as well as the Pushcart (2018—2020) and *Foreword* (2020) Prizes. His latest collection, *This House is Only a Nest* (Wayfarer Books 2024), is now available.

WHERE THE MUSIC COMES FROM

BY JOSE OSEGUERA

—for Luna

"She moved when I was playing guitar,"

my wife said, her palm flat on the copper strings.

As the life within her rippled beneath her rounded flesh,

I saw how our daughter interpreted the strange sounds

piercing through layers of muscle, fat

and water as melody—

music to be alive to.

I took the guitar from my wife

and plucked a melody from its body,

and I saw how my son slid his hand

into the hole past the vibrations,

the sound, the darkness,

unafraid of what might live in its depths.

He scratched the inner surface and smiled,

relieved to have finally discovered

where the music comes from.

TURTLE ISLAND
BY REBECCA DIETRICH

My roots run deep in this sacred land.
My ancestors lived and died here,
Long before the White man came.
"Our people met their people
when they got off the boat,"
As my grandfather used to say.
Yet we were the ones pushed around.
Gatsy was born in Georgia,
Her daughter Mahala in Oklahoma
And her daughter Buena too.
Grandpa Berry was born in Colorado
And my mother Nancy in Arizona.
She had me here in New Jersey.
When the time comes, I know
My children and their children
Will call Turtle Island home.

COLLAPSE
BY REBECCA DIETRICH

When the last drop of water is drunk,
The crops wither in their fields,
Lungs blacken from the falling ashes,
And the first innocent blood is spilled,
Will you still say it was worth it?

REBECCA DIETRICH (SHE/HER) is a Cherokee poet and photographer from Atlantic City, New Jersey. Her debut chapbook *Scholar of the Arts and Inhumanities* (Finishing Line Press, 2023) won the Literary Titan Book Award for Poetry. She has also published *The Last Lullaby* (Bottlecap Press, 2024) and *On Colonized Ground* (Alien Buddha Press, 2024). Dietrich's poetry has been published in *Red Coyote, Havik, Steam Ticket,* and elsewhere. She holds a B.A. in Psychology with a minor in Holocaust & Genocide Studies from Stockton University. Look for her next collection, *Under the Stars of Turtle Island*, is forthcoming from Wayfarer Books, April 2025.

A WORM IN SAVASANA, 2021

BY JACQUELINE HENRY

An earthworm stretches out on the concrete
and yawns, unaware of the crows pecking
in the grass nearby, hunting for
its kind of flesh.

      Does it hear their trilling?
Smell their need?
      That beaked hunger?

Or does it think that this moment of rest,
above ground, in the expanse of a summer morning,
with its blue sky and its moist sweetness
is worth the risk?

I am vigilant in my watching— from an old metal
rocker, white paint peeling off its sleeves—
blackbirds skirting my parents' yard like chickens
bobbing their heads looking for feed—

while the worm, in its blood-red blueness, peels itself
from the patio like Silly Putty, pebbled concrete
imprinted on its skin. It looks around, and once again,
lengthens.

      Why prostrate itself?
Is it unaware of the beaks? Or, uncaring?
      Is this a self sacrifice or a suicide?

It comes up out of the soil and into the bright,
and yet shades itself from singeing, bathing under
an old porous canopy my mother duct-taped
to four poles.

It must desire this life.
It must believe in its body. In its instinct and reflex,
in the regeneration of holy flesh

and confident too, that it can be seen only by those
doing a certain kind of watching.

*

I have to tell you: I don't know what became of it.

Later, I find my mother had dragged the iron chairs and the heavy glass
table around in a different direction. I knew then she had been thinking
about this all morning, the way she kept coming outside and staring as if
she were looking where I was looking but seeing something else unfold:
      How to sit. What to look at when sitting.

I would have told her: not how to sit but how to dive— deep
into a crevice and hide oneself in rocky stone.
I would have shown her how to wait, until evening, and rise up,
from darkness into blessed darkness.
      Into the fullness of embodied being—-

Stretching into Savasana,
Into the light of stars.

JACQUELINE HENRY (SHE/HER) is a Writer, Poet & Creative whose work has appeared in numerous literary magazines and publications. Under the name, Jackie Moloney, you'll find her teaching somatic writing, kundalini yoga and spirituality through her site Faith-in-Form.com. A Reiki Master and Embodied Yoga Life Coach, she offers distance Reiki sessions that harmonize energy healing with the art of writing. She is also a Reiki volunteer for her local hospice center.

EVENING BY THE RIVER

BY GARY WHITED

"People beside the river are watching the boats."
—David Ferry from "Down by the River"

The footbridge's arches look up at themselves
From the near perfect still water below,

As if completing their work for the day,
But of course they won't stop holding the bridge

Through the night for passersby to keep walking
Somewhere, wherever it is they are going

To be going. Odd how I take comfort
In knowing that I don't know, not in what

It is I don't know, but that it's there, as if
It meant to hold me up as I cross to where

It is I don't know I am going to.
Ya can't get there from here I'm told they say

Up in Maine when someone stops to ask for
Directions, and I nestle my want to know

Inside this little joke, or whatever it is,
And I don't even know what the joke means.

Maybe it's just an expression to tease
Someone wanting to get somewhere they don't

Know how to get to. Maybe, as David might say,
Something in us lives there inside the curve

Of that not knowing, and something we don't
Yet see glides through, that way a boat might pass

Beneath this bridge, maybe sometime in early
Morning, sometime when no one is here, as I am

Just now, to see it, and it won't ever
Be known, I guess, if no one sees it, but

Maybe a wake will ripple the water,
Signal that someone has slipped between

The curves of arch and arch looking up at itself,
An almost indiscernible glimpse into

What lives inside what we do not know—
That gate, we might say, to over there.

GARY WHITED (HE/HIM) is a poet, philosopher and psychotherapist. His first book titled, *Having Listened,* won the 2013 Homebound Publications Poetry Contest. In 2014 it received a Benjamin Franklin Silver Book Award, and in 2015 was translated into Russian and a bilingual edition was published. His second book, *Being, There* was published by Wayfarer Books in 2023. It includes new poems along with his translation of the ancient Greek fragments of Parmenides from the 5th century BCE. His poems have appeared in journals, including *Salamander, Plainsongs, The Aurorean, Atlanta Review, Comstock Review, The Wayfarer, Poetry Daily, The Red Letters* and *Kasparhauser.*

RETURNING TO AVERNO

BY C.W. EMERSON
—after Louise Glück

You die when your spirit dies.
You might stand up from a café table,
shift your weight onto a weakened hip,
and crumble like a scone, tumbling down
a flight of stairs. I remember the days
before my body betrayed me,
stepping smartly along Lexington
on my way to some meeting or event,
blithely bypassing others on the street,
so keen on my own self-importance.
I had plans, big plans, big ideas—
nothing seemed too far-fetched or
out of reach, so great was my certitude,
my sense of purpose. It was, to be sure,
the arrogance of youth, but essential
to the tasks which lay before me.
The decimation. I don't know how
to tell you this. I don't know whether
you need to know, or if you can even
empathize. I wanted to run out
into the street, scream no, no, no,
and I did, in my dreams. Now, I may
not know anymore the word for chair,
but I can sit happily in one for hours,
gazing out a random window, wool-
gathering, or watching people as they
come off the plane, vaguely dissociated,
time-obsessed, desperate for the next
text or call confirming their pick-up spot.
I was like that once, on the move,
a hunter, one of the pack. These days,
the young ones in white coats and sweats
nod, share glances they think I don't see,
ask me if I still practice. I tell them yes,
I still practice—that I am, in fact, at
the height of my powers.

C.W. EMERSON (HE/HIM), an award-winning poet, has received international recognition, including the C.P. Cavafy Poetry Prize (2018) and co-winner of the 2023-24 Poetry International Summer Chapbook competition. His work, often exploring themes relevant to LGBTQIA+ communities, has appeared in *Harvard Review, Oxford University Press,* and *Tupelo Quarterly.* Emerson is the author of *Off Coldwater Canyon* (2021), *The Thoracic Diaries* (forthcoming), and *Danger Face* (2025), winner of the 2024 Homebound Poetry Prize. A retired clinical psychologist, he divides his time between southern California and San Miguel de Allende, Mexico. Visit theolderamericanpoet.com.

BOY BY THE BOGACIEL
BY WALKER ABEL

Great presences coalesce out of mist, out of forest

time bends in on itself like dunking one's head in a river

and realizing no sense of length, dreams are visions

of what might be and what is, is distillations of dreams:

a boy holding an owl between his outstretched fingers

the owl looking at me without concern

born there in the fragrance of that suspension

the poised being of a flower stem-held among ferns

a pebble single as a first star shining from the river floor.

The boy's young friends toe their sneakers in the duff

smiling that he always does this, not doubting the story

that a snake came first to his side, then the owl

to catch or join the snake, and he gathered up the bird

as the turning earth does its seasons, as sky folds in

its clouds and without strain makes each feel welcome.

Fifty years now have passed or been plucked

as melody from the lute. If ever you read this

you boy now man, please send me a feather

a verse, an uplifting shape in the swirls of dream

that you still walk and sing by the river.

WHAT HAPPENS
TO A DAY THAT HAS PASSED?
BY WALKER ABEL

You spent it, say, hiking over desert hills –

the flowers of spring; clouds swim by

the scales of an immeasurable fish.

The day, all of it, came in through the eyes

through the nose, the ears, the mouth.

The feet minutely took in the day, the hands as well.

When the sun has set and twilight come

it seems the whole day like an ocean

has sunk slowly, and you wonder

where it flowed, what hidden chamber

of your body now holds all that water.

For surely nothing is ever lost

and your experience of a day, however private

goes somewhere, and the desert's experience

you part of it, goes somewhere.

And so it is as the moon rises, you lay your head

on the unknowable ground of countless oceans

pouring down one funnel to the same place.

WALKER ABEL (HE/HIM) has published four volumes of poetry, all with Wayfarer Books. His poems spring from the two fundamental influences of his adult life: decades of intimacy with wilderness areas of the West, and decades of engagement with the practices and teachings within Taoism and Zen Buddhism.

RAMSHACKLE INN

BY ROBERT BRODER

Tony Periwinkle is a large man
who meticulously designs and builds miniatures.
He loves the smell of
sawdust,
the rhythm of his
jigsaw,
and the sound of
sandpaper
smoothing out the tiniest of objects.
At the moment, he is tinkering on Ramshackle Inn.
The lobby looks grand,
even though it is small,
Tony cracks ceramic tiles
to design a mosaic for the foyer,
carefully placing each chipped piece into place.
The banister that winds up to the second and third floor
are twisted twigs he finds while hiking in the woods
with Low-Rider, his trusty Basset Hound.
When needed
he takes his weathered flannel shirts
and methodically snips and sews
the smallest of items for each room.
Curtains,
linens,
and rugs
all have a touch of plaid.

Clay is molded into toilets,
sinks
and clawfoot tubs,
then bisque-fired until they are bright white.
Using rubber-tipped tongs,
Tony sets them into each bathroom.
He manipulates
empty soup cans with needle-nose pliers
to cut and bend the aluminum
to make room keys, silverware, and chandeliers.
He grabs his magnifying glass and inspects Ramshackle Inn.
"Almost finished," he says to himself.

After a long day, Tony and Low-Rider
take a walk along the ridge and look out at the town together.
Tomorrow, Tony will gently melt clear wine bottles and craft a "No Vacancy"
sign.

ROBERT BRODER (HE/HIM) is a picture book author and developmental editor. He likes hiking, snow, dogs, and coffee—preferably all four at once, in his favorite flannel shirt. Robert lives with his family in a small town, near a big lake, surrounded by green mountains. RobertBroder.com

YOUR MOTHER WAS YOUNG—
BY REBECCA BRENNER

barely over the shock of you.
A daughter with wounds
stitched over creation.

She fumbled breasts

into your small, searching mouth
unsure what they would give—
her mind a menace.

A tattered cloth heirloom handed down,

tangled threads from her mother,
and her mother before.
She loved you with quaking bones,

hoping you would know.
And you—small and wise—
felt it seep through her skin,

understood the weight of things

before you knew the words for them.
And you drank that love,
terrestrial waters, sweet and bitter both,

embracing the weight of this life,

unable to destroy the world's origins
set deep into your marrow,

silent and true.

A MARRIAGE
BY REBECCA BRENNER

that doesn't hold the same shape forever
isn't a failure—
this illumination is not an accident.
A ring taken off is a
soft, yet definite clearness of
air where something solid used to be,
gentle space redefining its edges.

Between us now—
bodies that never conceptualize themselves,
we allow what is—
atoms placed randomly then further apart,
orbiting in their quiet pull,
moving, not lost.
Together or alone, I'm told,
we can still close our eyes and see God.

I'M IN A HOUSE

BY REBECCA BRENNER

that is a mix of my current home,
North Heide Lane and Roosevelt Avenue.

I'm in my bed, Mom is in the hallway.

I follow her down the stairs
through the kitchen into a basement
and through the cellar door.

We're standing near a field that opens out onto the ocean.

She looks healthy, peaceful.
I ask if she is happy
about our writing.

She says yes and takes my hand.

The wind and waves pick up.
She's gone.
I can feel the aliveness of it all—

how we're all, it's all a process unfolding.

I feel connected to the process,
connected to my place in the lineage of mothers.
But mostly I'm glad I can finally feel her in my heart again.

REBECCA BRENNER (SHE/HER), author and mindfulness meditation teacher, has been featured in *TIME, LA Times*, and *Tin House*. A journalist for *TownLift*, she co-founded *Mindful*. Summit County and serves on Summit Pride's Leadership Team. Her memoir-in-verse, *Paper House*, debuts with Wayfarer Books in Summer 2025.

AUTUMNAL DETENTION CENTER

BY GWENDOLYN MORGAN

"ICE finds itself bedeviled
by activists, attorneys
and politicians in the Pacific Northwest
who are determined to gum up
the machines of immigrant enforcement."

She remembers that a grateful heart
illuminates the space around it.

Underneath feathered clouds
she waits outside
the Immigration Detention Center.

With mothers from around the world
she leans against the cement wall
cries for her children.

Above rare "blue" (Snow Geese)
mostly dark bodies and wings
issue high-pitched laments.

TRAUMA-INFORMED CARE

BY GWENDOLYN MORGAN

No estas sola
she is a resident of a state
"diametrically opposed to
the national policies of enforcement
resisting immigration practices
that are espousing
human rights violations."

She says they need to stop disorientation
stop separation of parents from children
as she keeps social distance

even geese know better
how to care for their young
a grateful heart illuminates

trauma-informed care
fluorescent lights overhead
she watches the seasonal migration

of birds, farm workers, retraumatization
repeat: "What do our
descendants ask of us?"

GWENDOLYN MORGAN (SHE/HER) is a Pacific Northwest poet and artist who has served in interfaith spiritual care in medical centers for nearly two decades. She learned the names of birds and inherited horsehair paint brushes and wooden paint boxes from her grandmothers. She is a recipient of a few residencies including a Centrum Artist Residency. The Clark County Poet Laureate 2018-2020 in Washington State, her third book of poetry, *Before the Sun Rises* (Wayfarer Books) is a Nautilus Silver Winner in Poetry. As a multiracial family in a multi-species watershed, they are committed to equity work and inclusion for all.

LIGHT, SOUND, BONE

GWENDOLYN MORGAN

Hermit Thrush, Swainson's Thrush
flutelike   intricate inspirations
elaborations   embroidered embellishments
variations from established climate patterns

vibrations of notes, patterns, shiny shells, buttons
produced by the syrinx in the windpipe
peace pipe   grouse   snipe
woodcock   nighthawk   everyone vocal

drumming of Acorn Woodpecker on hollow tree
she rises on thermals, prevailing winds from the west
from the ocean, over the Cascade Range
nothing feels the same, looks the same

Tundra Swan feathers   Snow Goose feathers
Golden Eagle feathers   Raven feathers
how the wind lifts the bones   the melodies
vibrations of light, sound, bone

how to be a hollow bone, naming birds, weather patterns
how to let the wind speak through her sorrow
how to protest the violence, environmental destruction
hurricane, tornado, tsunami

sound a gesture
a song   one found consonant
release adjective, adverb, torrential sorrow
sign another petition, stand in the rain of her precinct

unprecedented monsoon rains in the Pacific Northwest
she takes organic non-gmo heirloom seeds into her teeth
sends songs to Greta Thunberg, her grandchildren
immigrant children on the borderlands

blue songs   blue star niños
ultra-violet violet-blue
intrasolar   interlunar   interplanetary aura of
imaginary wings and memories

she bones her way across centuries of poverty, protest
carries melodies of what it means to care for the earth
dawning awareness
before the birds sing

before the first sign of light
she remembers how to be vocal.

RAID PEAK ACCORDING TO STONE SWIMMER
by Michael Garrigan

Every place has a valley just over its crest few
venture into it. Most people only follow the trails,
turning back when they end, relying only on sight.

Follow water to its root, climb towards the horizon
until Raid Peak punctures it. Wander and amble
back and forth down the steep topography towards

the base of the mountain. There, look up, trace
the alpine bloodclot lichen and seams of gneiss
until you find us on the ridge, tumbling into sky.

EPISTEMOLOGY: ESTUARY
by Michael Garrigan

A melding stillness—
her feet sunken firm in this small
estuary where creek meets ocean;

seaweed and small stones painted with root blood,
creeping dogwood in sand around her ankles, spruce
holding wind even when water is flat calm at her back.

She watches brook trout coast in on high tide
chased by some larger fish—stripers maybe?
would they eat something so beautiful?—

and marvels at how they hold the soft color of salt
around each faint halo and how their skin maps tides
and currents and how one mineral can change a body.

MICHAEL GARRIGAN (HE/HIM) writes and teaches
along the Susquehanna River in Pennsylvania. He is
the author of the poetry collections *River, Amen* and
Robbing the Pillars. He was an Artist in Residence for
The Bob Marshall Wilderness Area and you can find
more of his work at www.mgarrigan.com.

STARTLED INTO FLAME
by Janna Knittel

a grouse exploded
from underbrush,
comet of feathers

and fear. Alone
on the Grand Portage
I leapt backwards:

As a kid
in Oregon deserts,
I'd trained myself

to brace and listen
for rattlesnakes.
Though I'd sweated

through my khaki
shirt and pants
and longed

for cold shower, colder
beer, I hung
a moment, finding

how to breathe
the sodden air,
wishing Grouse

and I could share
a laugh, how I
mistook a bird

for venomous snake,
how it took me
for creature

who would dare
pull one gold
or russet feather

let alone harm
the promises
in its nest.

THE LAST CORMORANT
by Janna Knittel

A double-crested cormorant balances
on a buoy, drapes its wings over water
to drip-dry. Dracularian silhouette,
standing strong as wind shakes sailboats'
sails like gauze. A white-tailed kite flies,
spear-straight, crying chee chee chee chee,
to settle and shelter among lashing leaves.
Bring boats in to dock. Evening walks
quickly, and quicker, past the equinox.

JANNA KNITTEL (PRONOUN PREFERENCE: USE NAME) is the author of *Real Work* (Nodin, 2022), a finalist for the 2023 Minnesota Book Award in poetry, and the chapbook *Fish & Wild Life* (Finishing Line, 2018). Janna has also published poems in *Blue Mountain Review, Conduit, Constellations, North Dakota Quarterly, Pleiades, The Trumpeter*, and *The Wild Word* as well as the following anthologies: *Waters Deep: A Great Lakes Anthology* (Split Rock, 2018); *The Experiment Will Not Be Bound* (Unbound Edition, 2023); and *Broad Wings, Long Legs: A Rookery of Heron Poems* (North Star, 2024).

THANK YOU

Thank you for purchasing this issue of

Wayfarer Magazine

At *Wayfarer Magazine*, our journey has always been guided by a deep passion for storytelling, exploration, and connecting with kindred spirits like you. Your unwavering support, curiosity, and shared love for independent voices make everything we do possible. Every page we craft, every story we tell, and every adventure we celebrate is fueled by your encouragement. Thank you for walking this path with us and believing in our mission to inspire, inform, and ignite the spirit of wanderlust. Together, we'll continue to explore the uncharted. Here's to many more journeys ahead!

BIG SUR, CALIFORNIA
BY CONNOR WOLFE

FOLLOW US

 www.facebook.com/thewayfarermagazine

 www.instagram.com/thewayfarer__mag/

 www.instagram.com/wayfarer.books

ABIQUIÚ, NEW MEXICO | BY CONNOR WOLFE